This Way Up: Remembering Who We Are

by Wendy Mandy

Love

Wendy.

Copyright © Wendy Mandy 2021

Edited by Nick Johnstone

Painting by Jesse Jewel Pigott
Design by Manon Prost

Published by Mallhouse Press

978-1-915292-23-0

This book is dedicated to all children and all indigenous tribes for helping me remember who we truly are.

Special thanks to my children Jesse and Angelica and my grandchildren Elektra and Juno, my niece Iris and my nephew Gabriel.

Author's Note

I decided to call this book *This Way Up*. The title came to me, guided. I woke in the middle of the night and asked for inspiration. Getting out of bed to walk outside and look at the moon, I tripped over a bag on which was written the words: This Way Up. The second part - *Remembering Who We Are* - is about sharing knowledge that I have received from tribes about our place in nature and through lived experience and tens of thousands of hours spent healing clients and studying alternative medicine. *This Way Up i*s also about reaching for the stars with our feet firmly on the earth, a mantra of sorts, I live by.

In more than forty years of work, I have treated clients all over the world with and trained in Herbal Medicine, Gardening, Land Healing, Feng Shui, Peruvian, Celtic and African Shamanism, Homeopathy, Reflexology, Massage, Shiatsu, Weather Shamanism, Distance Healing, Traditional Chinese Medicine, 5-Element Acupuncture, Sexual Abuse Counselling and Addiction Therapy.

I have lived and travelled all over the world and lost my worldly goods several times. I feel this has contributed to my understanding of how we can hold a more truthful relationship to each other and nature. It is my belief that we can learn so much about other ways of living by listening to the wisdom of Indigenous people who have not been taken over by monotheistic religion. Tribal structures and Indigenous behaviour around family, sexuality and community can teach us so much. The present moment which is always now offers us all the possibilities to upgrade our collective energetic state, if we are open to it.

I have been working in this field most of my life and I always experience people wanting to know who they really are deep down in their heart. The key to understanding ourselves goes beyond the self. It's about rediscovering the universal, the indigenous within us all. We are all one. Rediscovering this wisdom is essential if we are to find a better way to live. This book brings together a lifetime of learning and it is my pleasure to share it with you.

– Wendy Mandy, Bath, Somerset, U.K, 2021

1

My adventures around this beautiful planet and my continuous inner journey of remembering who we really are tells me we can tune in more positively to life, if we can find a rhythm with each other and nature.

I would like to inspire you as I have been inspired by visiting indigenous tribes, to know we can make a difference in society through cooperation, peace and love. The ups and downs of our lives and the internal and external journeys are still there of course, because, just like nature, we are constantly flowing and changing.

There is a coherence of connection that makes sense of life, whether it's easy or difficult on that particular day. It's this intrinsic quality of connectedness with all things that has been lost for a very long time, leaving us confused and stranded in a world of separation and duality that causes conflict.

Rediscovering ourselves is often the answer to most modern maladies. We all have the power to free ourselves from the structures and systems of living that we have manifested together from the concept of duality.

Duality permeates our society in every way until it becomes so familiar we no longer see it. To explain what duality is, we need to understand what Taoism is. Taoism is the constant flow of opposites, light and dark, male and female, and duality is where these opposites become separated. Over time we have been led to believe in the separation of light and dark, them and us, which in turn leads to a whole host of problems like codependence and unnecessary competition that we deal with today. I believe that through creating a form of living where duality has no place, we can find true happiness through self-acceptance, purpose, connectedness and flow.

From a grounded place, we are always reaching for the stars. We are a precious package that needs self care as we journey through the often rough terrain of life. I believe that in all of us sits the complete understanding of everything that the universes have to offer. We only have to remember how to access the knowledge that lives in the present, the past and the future.

We are but a moment in time.

Once you step into the journey of understanding yourself, there is no going back. Even though ignorance sometimes feels like bliss, there is a nagging feeling of incompleteness when we are not acting from a place of connection with our deepest self and source.

Many years of connecting with indigenous people has taught me that most of the answers we crave in the Western world can be found by remembering we are a part of nature. I believe we can take inspiration from the way humans used to live in tribes before organised religion and large civilisations became the norm. Somewhere along the line we have lost the ability to feel connected in the moment to all that is.

However, because we are so blinded by our own perspective and our own egoistic sense of certainty, we often can't see Indigenous wisdom for what it is. We mis-perceive the ancient ways, take them out of context and view them through the only filter we know: the world as we see it and have been conditioned to see it. In doing this, we risk losing the potential for broadening our understanding.

In my visits to the Samburu tribe, who live in Laikipia, Kenya, I have witnessed well meaning tourists say things like, 'They are so poor, how can we help them?', when in reality the real help we can give is to leave them alone. The undoubtedly well meaning comment from the tourist calls into question what it means to be poor. What is poverty anyway? The Samburu may not have a wealth of material possessions as we define them in the modern world, but they have enormous spiritual and environmental wealth. They really know what inner happiness is, that comes from the security of knowing their place in the cosmos. They know they are meant to be who they are in the environment they are in. They are unconditionally loved by their word for God or the creator and by their family or tribe.

We are constantly questioning our existence, how we look, and how we relate as we have been brought up to be competitive with each other rather than cooperative with each other. We now live in a very individualistic society in which we feel lonely because we can never be satisfied because there is never enough. We are all different. Some of us like to be leaders and some not. Society is made up of many different characters who appreciate each others' differences.

I asked a Samburu friend who lives with his seven wives, who all support each other and laugh together, 'How do you celebrate birthdays?'

He replied, 'We don't celebrate birthdays because everyday is a birthday with a gift from nature. Everyday is a special day in its own way.'

Before the British arrived in Kenya, the Samburu lived simply with cows, goats, camels, grass, herbs and everything that their livestock gave them. They had skins for clothes and shelter, dung to build the houses with and milk from the livestock. They would mix the milk with blood from a little nick in the neck of the animal that they made after stroking the animal into a relaxed state. They would then heal the wound with a poultice of herbs. This was a complete food of unpasteurised milk full of goodness with the vitamins and minerals from the blood.

Even today, after much Western infiltration and tampering, they never show any cruelty when they host a ceremony involving an animal. They choose an animal, commune with its soul and soothe it with gentle stroking and then expertly kill it with no pain or trauma. Everything they do is with reverence and by default sustainable. When they move camp they leave no trace. They only use fallen down bushes or trees as shelter or firewood. Their water comes from the rivers. Their approach to life is hugely inspiring. The abundance of an uninterfered nature fills them with gratitude every day.

I attended an Australian corroboree (Aboriginal traditional dance ceremony) when I lived in Queensland in the early Nineties. Historically, Aboriginal Australians had an extremely sophisticated relationship to the land which involved tuning in to all its landmarks and frequencies in a completely respectful way. They had no need to build shelters as they moved around the landscape grouped in what they called a mob.

At night, the women, the men and the children slept in a huddle to keep warm and they knew - in what to us would be a barren landscape - where to find food. They never over-ran or over-hunted an area, keeping a very close relationship with every living thing. When colonists arrived, they hunted and killed the Aboriginal peoples and quickly destroyed absolutely everything about their sophisticated understanding of nature.

2

We would all be so much happier if we were able to succinctly and fearlessly work out why our lives are not harmonious. Too often we have to reach a place of acute discomfort to make change, for example a health scare, an accident or a significant illness. But it doesn't have to come from a place of shock, a spiritual jolt or trauma. It can come more simply from the pursuit and realisation of meaningful self-awareness.

I have always followed my heart. After spending much time across my life with Indigenous people, such as the Samburu, who have not been under the yoke of the duality of religion, I know we can live happier and less burdened lives. I've seen it with my own eyes.

The most important members of any indigenous community are children. To raise children in integrity we should first do our very best to heal our inner child. Parts of us easily become traumatised as we grow up, especially in the early years from conception to the age of three.

Gabor Maté, the celebrated trauma specialist, has written many books on trauma, the most famous being *In the Realm of Hungry Ghosts*. In his books he explains how children arrive into the world biologically preprogrammed to form attachments to others to survive.

The famous psychoanalyst, John Bowlby, echoes this research, suggesting the child has an innate need to attach to one main attachment figure in the critical years of birth to three years old. Maternal deprivation observes that the continual disruption between infant and primary care givers can result in emotional, cognitive and social difficulties. Maté observed that in addicts of all types, the original attachment of the addict to the primary caregiver had been disrupted.

Jean Liedloff, author of *The Continuum Concept,* who spent time with the Yequana Amazonian tribe, observed that the children of the tribe did not cry, complain or act out because they were in a caring supportive social structure. And that each mother was supported to be with her child. My own visits to Indigenous tribes have convinced me that the overall health of the adult comes back to how secure, attached and loved the baby is from conception to three years old.

One snowy Sunday, Jean Liedloff came for lunch at our house on Portobello Road. My eldest daughter was two and a half years old. Jean decided she wanted to go for a walk among the snow-covered stalls of Portobello Market. I went to get warm clothes for my daughter who flatly refused to put any on.

Jean said, "Let's just go and bring her clothes in a basket".

Off we trotted down the road, with me walking at least twenty five yards behind this very tall woman and a naked toddler. Even though people stared, she walked on regardless. It was only when we got to Golborne Road, half an hour away, that Jesse asked for her clothes. She was perfectly well and showed no signs then or after of being cold despite the snow. I learnt that day to believe children at all times in regard to their personal choice over what they wanted to wear.

Trauma is often created unintentionally by well meaning parents leaving their children to cry, imagining it would create independence long before a child is able to understand what independence means. Independence comes naturally, when a child feels secure and the parent feels secure enough to let the baby go exploring when they learn to walk because they know they have given the child the appropriate amount of love before this.

One of my clients had a baby with a member of a tribe in the Amazon rainforest. He wanted to take the child and the mother of the child back to the U.K. She refused to leave her tribe. Three and a half years later the mother appeared in London without the child. When he asked her where his child was, she answered, "I was with the baby for the first three years as the mother, and now the baby is with the tribe." She knew she had given that baby her appropriate attention surrounded by a loving, supportive team and that she could now go away for a visit without traumatising the baby. She also knew that the baby's needs would not be met in a nuclear family lacking the community infrastructure, warmth and protection of a tribe in a big city.

Later on in life, trauma can be activated like an alarm bell we have no control over by situations that we perceive as similar to when we were very young or perhaps pre-verbal. To raise children properly it is advisable for us to heal these parts within us. It's an obvious thing to say but knowing yourself fully makes child rearing less dramatic, less painful and more enjoyable.

If you already have children that you have raised without fully understanding yourself - and you will know if this is you as you read these words - it is never too late to change those patterns by seeking out a new level of self awareness. Obviously it is harder if the relationships with your children have become fractured and difficult, but if you persevere the most extraordinary patterns can be changed and all the old difficulties can potentially disappear. Damage is never set in stone. I've witnessed the most extraordinary reparations between parents and their children if underlying anger is finally resolved. And I always encourage people to attempt to repair relationships with their family as a pattern of conflict will otherwise continue with new intimate relationships.

Like all parents, I have made mistakes with my children and I have learnt what I know today the hard way. However, I have noticed with both my children and my grandchildren and other children that have come through my life that, if I can identify the source of the original problem, harmony can be restored very easily.

If you take responsibility for your part in any conflict and apologise, the conflict is easily dispersed. If I sense discomfort in anyone around me, including in plants or animals, which I feel in my body, physically, I check myself immediately.

Sometimes discomfort turns up as an uncomfortable energy between myself and a stranger which is palpable. As I am the creator of my perception I make sure I am not available for any transfer of another person's discomfort by staying centred and sometimes shifting my position physically, for example, by breathing more deeply.

For example, if I am busy parking my car and in doing so, blocking the road and another driver is trying to get past me, making signs he or she is in a hurry, I make sure I straighten up immediately to let them pass. This gesture dispels their aggression. I have no desire to be the one they are angry with. Kindness breaks their spell and they mostly will respond by acknowledging my efforts with gratitude.

I also check myself and as I breathe, run a quick inventory to see if I may have attracted any possible aggression in the first place. This all may sound like hard work but entering into another's negative transference is much harder work as it creates so much confusion and misery. Knowing yourself creates relief and flow in the present.

I saw a wonderful example of how to repair a relationship when I visited a Brazilian tribe. There were two teenagers in the tribe who I noticed did nothing all day, except hang around and it intrigued me that no one seemed to tell them off or ask them to spend their time more meaningfully. When I asked the Chief why this was, he replied that they had not decided what they wanted to do with their days yet.

It is the Indigenous way to lead and show by example rather than issue instruction, which they believe will only make a person more resistant. He later told me that something had happened to their father which caused them to lose motivation. By allowing them space, they felt able to do nothing.

On my next visit, I noticed they were as motivated as all the other members of the tribe. It is our expectation of others around us that often leads to conflict and we often just need to leave space for people to be who they are and work it out for themselves.

3

I truly believe the company we keep and how we relate to that company influences our day to day experience and mindset. You can find yourself waiting at a bus stop in pouring rain and feeling good about yourself and life and as a by-product, the people around you too. Or you can be staying on a beautiful island and having a terrible time because of how you feel inside and this too will affect how you feel about the people around you. Our mind states and moods radiate out and perception is coloured accordingly.

Outside perception and inside perception is always a mirror. When people truly understand themselves, they automatically see that the only way to live is open-heartedly rather than through the intellectual self. Life is about ups and downs, easy times and more difficult times – this is how we learn.

One must always look at nature and see how she operates. Nothing is fixed in nature, and surprise is around every corner. In a garden you can prepare the soil with organic compost, plant your seeds with love, water them and tend to them carefully. However, the outcome of each plant's growth and its resilience to rain, cold and bright sun wildly varies.

You soon learn plants have an individual way of responding to their environment and you learn to live with life and death in a different way. If you walk in the wild you will notice a buzzard suddenly swooping on a hapless furry fluffy dormouse and devouring it. Do you sympathise with the dormouse or the buzzard? Who is in the moral, environmental right, the dormouse or the buzzard, or are they in a symbiosis with each other with no judgement?

Through my work with clients struggling with everything from depression, anxiety, sleep disturbance and digestive problems to self-loathing, loss of meaning and purpose, one thing has become clear to me: we do not understand happiness in the Western world. Despite the explosion of self-help literature from the Sixties onwards and the recent boom in the wellness sector and industry, we are arguably more unhappy than we have ever been.

So many of the clients I see have problems with compulsive and addictive behaviour. One of the most common and socially acceptable forms of addiction is workaholism, which is an infection of the body, mind and spirit in its purest form. But there's a paradox here too – while we've all been conditioned to accept that success takes graft, when it comes to changing ourselves and our relationships, we are so impatient.

Many people come to me hoping for a quick fix to their unhappiness or suffering. They think they can attend a single session and duck out of doing the hard work. They are disappointed when I explain to them this is not possible. This is because working on our relationship with ourselves and with other people takes time, patience and effort. It is a process, a life's work with which we need to engage again and again. The impact of good relationships extends to our physical, mental and spiritual health. It amplifies across the social and economic spectrum, powering good to infinity.

4

My time on this planet began when I was born in Malaysia in 1951 to an aristocratic mother and an army officer father. Soon after my birth, we moved to Nigeria and I spent the first five years of life there. My early childhood in Africa had a profound effect on my trust in people and nature. I had a happy time with the loving African people who cared for me. Returning to England, I went to a private prep school, where I missed the warmth of my early Malaysian and African caregivers.

Without question, I knew I was a healer from a very young age. I used to make 'Wendy houses' in the garden and mix spells and potions from different plants, stones, feathers and so on. No one taught me to make spells and potions, except perhaps my mother who understood nature very well.

I learned about witches in fairy tales and knew in my heart there were good and bad witches. I liked making mixtures out of natural things and felt they were powerful if you put your wishes into them. Some of this came from having been partly raised in Africa where belief and faith in magic and superstition is abundant.

By the time I was making spells and potions, I was running wild in a very pretty village in England that had not yet been modernised. In my young eyes, nature seemed very much alive. On top of this, I remember feeling different and alone even though I was an extremely sociable child.

My parents let me roam freely and explore nature and I started to read her ways of teaching. I found solace in the rhythms of nature. And if I was lost on my pony, I would ask a tree how to find my way home. Not everyone will understand this, but I'm perfectly serious when I say I have always felt the language of trees. They feel still, patient and wise, whatever we do to them. I would ask the tree a question and the answer would appear in my heart. The tree would confirm my instinct with a yes or no feeling.

I enjoyed churches not for the teachings but for the acoustics of the building and the peace and quiet created for meditation. I would go in there when no one was around and pick primroses for my mother that grew in the graveyard. I used to love the church bells and felt transported into other worlds by their sound. I use singing bowls in my treatment room and have always instinctively known how to play them. My favourite is an ancient Tibetan bowl I bought in a night market in Beijing once.

Even though I was a child, I knew I was tapping into some other information because I could heal plants and small animals that I would find like wounded birds or half eaten mice. For example, I would bring home a wounded bird if it couldn't fly. My mother was also very good at rescuing small creatures. Usually though they were past the point of no return and over time, I made a graveyard of sorts in the garden.

From an early age, I had a clear sixth sense as we often call it and knew what people were thinking and before I had learnt tact would say things in public like, 'Mummy, that woman doesn't like us'.

I also had the ability to intuitively know who was what I would now call possessed. I could feel if a person had a darker energy controlling them. My mother had a friend who I considered very dark and she plagued my childhood. As I was a child, I was still very much in touch with my feelings and was very aware that my mother seemed to change when this woman was in the room. This woman appeared to look after my mother and the illusion of support seemed to cloud my mother's normally good judgement. I could sense this woman was jealous of me as her daughter was a year younger than me and she emanated the impression that she believed I overshadowed her daughter. She would make very critical comments that turned my mother against me and even at that age I knew that my tight stomach and beating heart signified danger as my primary caretaker was being unduly influenced to turn away from me, threatening my safety.

These days, if I encounter a person in or out of my treatment room that appears to behave in a negative way, I have many tools with 5-Element Acupuncture or shamanism to remove the dark energy in their auric field or around them that can be deep or superficial.

If it's deep, it may be a split in their personality and energy field going right back even to the womb or it could be a recent discordant energy that they have picked up in their auric field by perhaps excess addiction or a relationship with somebody toxic. I have learned to smile and shine light at anything dark until it shrivels up and leaves. A psychic once told me I was very protected and that anyone who attacked me would fall on their own sword.

As I entered double digit years as a child, I read any book I could find on nature, magic, other cultures and knew that later on, my version of studying at university was going to be travel.

Having spent the first five years of my life away from a classroom and the tight smallness of English life, I knew I wanted to experience as soon as possible the colours, smells and flavours of other cultures and what they could teach you.

Through books and encyclopaedias I read, I came to know there was a whole world out there that I wanted to experience rather than be told about. All my instincts went towards the wish for experience as a learning tool.

Education even though it was more project based when I was a child, leaned towards being a right or a wrong answer to a question rather than a healthy debate.

My parents encouraged me to think for myself and to be free. Being short of money, they were delighted that I would want to be financially self-sufficient and always gave me the impression that they thought that I was perfectly capable of looking after myself. Having travelled widely themselves, they gave me the impression that seeing the world and interacting with different cultures was a great education.

My grandmother gave me money to start my travels when I was a teenager. The first place I went abroad was Portugal. I went with a boyfriend when I was fourteen.

A year later, aged fifteen, I went to France on a language exchange programme and lived with a very large, very eccentric French family. In those days no one was watching you or photographing you so you felt free to learn each day from the successes and mistakes of your adventures. I always say to young people, despite the incessant background recording on Instagram, Facebook, Snapchat, Twitter and the looming realities of the Metaverse, Dance as though no one is watching.

At the end of my stay with the French family, I decided to join one of my young friends who was a boy but not a boyfriend and we had a nasty encounter with a lorry driver who tried to take off with just me in his cab. Using basic self defence I managed to hit him hard enough that the lorry slowed down enough for me to jump out and roll onto the side of the road. Shell shocked, I found my friend and being an eternal optimist, I knew we would be alright, and to my delight round the next corner found that he had thrown all our possessions out onto the road. I learned from this encounter to be free but not put myself in unnecessary danger.

Separated from my friend and travelling alone, I realised at the Italian border that I did not have my passport. A kind passport official took me to his home where he lived with his mother and I telephoned my father using reverse charges and asked him to phone my French host family and ask if they had found my passport left behind and if they did, could they please send it to me poste restante as close as possible to the Italian family I was staying with. This all took about six days and I learned a lot about trust and that people are kind in the most peculiar places. I also learned a valuable lesson thereafter to always know where my passport is at all times as the French family had found it under the bed I was sleeping in. My suggestion to anyone is to know that when things appear to go wrong to work out what you need to learn and then with a little more humility and the wish to grow, life goes back into flow.

In parallel with these debut travel experiences, I became obsessed with first nation North American culture. This passion was ignited when I found a book of pictures of first nation American people by the photographer Edward Curtis in a library. Everything about their lives, for example how they lived in a tipi, made sense to me. Because of my early observations of how local Nigerians lived, I felt communal living in natural structures was a positive way to live.

Alongside the photos, when I read the words of first nation people and their reverence for mother nature, something stirred in me. My connection to these people and their way of life was so eerily strong that I wondered immediately if I had experienced life in a tipi in another incarnation because I felt I knew exactly what it was like to lie on the ground next to my tribe looking up at the poles meeting in the middle and the smoke of the fire curling upwards through the slit in the ceiling.

Overnight, my perspective changed. Living in a concrete box with a stressed mother and an absent working father and often angry siblings next to other stressed families seem nonsensical. By contrast, the faces in Curtis' photographs were so beautiful and possessed a deep wisdom, also calmness and love.

5

I left school at 16 and moved to London. I answered an ad in *The Times* that read: 'Assistant Editor wanted for International magazine'. I rang the telephone number from a phone box. A man answered and wouldn't give me any information except to tell me to come to a particular address in Paddington at 8 pm the same day. I arrived at 8pm and noticed there were only young women in the queue which I thought was slightly peculiar. I made my way through the queue and at the front door a couple of hippies were sitting surrounded by paper.

I joined them sitting on the floor and said, "So what's the job?" and they laughed and said: "There is no job. We don't have any money".

"But this looks fun", I replied. "Why did you put the ad in the paper then?".

"I didn't. Richard did".

It seems unfathomable to process this scene today but 'Richard' was Richard Branson and Virgin was about to enter existence as a small business.

We chatted and I convinced them to let me return the next morning. And so it was, I started working for Richard Branson the following morning and went on to work on many interesting projects, developing the mail order offering by Virgin Records, opening the first Virgin record shop above a shoe shop on Oxford Street and then the opening of the Virgin studio and the Virgin Records label office.

Richard was flexible, so I could disappear for two or three months at a time and go travelling and thoroughly enjoy myself and then come back to a new assignment. He was also very good at delegating, and he taught me three skills that I have today. He taught me that there is no such thing as a mistake, only experience, that all publicity is good publicity because you learn from it and that you must go through your edge to truly live.

Richard set up an organisation called Help and my role was counselling pregnant young women. There was a huge problem with STDs and unwanted pregnancies. Most often I was taking care of Irish girls flocking to England for abortions. Some girls though had been raped. They would call in response to our Help leaflet which was the only way we had of advertising at the time and I would answer the phone. They would bring a urine sample to the door which I would label and then take to a lab in South London. In the afternoon I'd ring for the results and it was my job to break the news to the girls. I would then arrange for a proper hospital abortion for the pregnant ones, often taking them home afterwards to my flat. Through this, I realised I had a counselling skill. I'd also offer them Reflexology treatments and notice the benefits it gave them.

At one point in the life of Virgin Records, we had to leave Richard's mother's comfortable home as we had so little money and recast our offices in the crypt of a local church. My counselling desk was a tombstone illuminated by candlelight.

In my work helping the pregnant girls, I came to realise I had a psychic sense too of what was troubling them and that it helped me to pinpoint early trauma leading to consequences in their life. Through them, I also had my first experiences of holding ceremonies around birth and death. I would hold their hand and help them understand the trauma of losing a baby.

Fifteen years later, I attended an African ceremony hosted by teacher and writer Sobonfu Somé in Burkina Faso, where ninety traumatised women who had never expressed grief around miscarriage and abortion, were led through a very healing ceremony. Whatever we have to do that is difficult in life, doing it with support ceremony and compassion takes away trauma, guilt and shame.

With that light turned on, I began my path into studying healing modalities. I started with Shiatsu because I had been reading about Taoism and Acupuncture meridians which led me in turn to be very interested in the concept of 'we are what we eat'.

I took a year-long course on herbal medicine, as herbs can have an influence not just on the body but on the mind, spirit and emotions. I also realised I had to learn a protocol for healing that would set safe and secure boundaries with the people I was helping.

When I was nineteen, I had my first encounter with a First Nation American near Death Valley in California who told me I would become an 'Eagle Woman'. Along with saying this, he gave me a necklace of turquoise and a bone eagle which I went on to wear for years, before losing it sometime in my late Twenties.

I met him not long after visiting the Grand Canyon with Nik Powell, Richard Branson's original partner in Virgin Records, and my first husband, Steve Mandy. We were all in the States on a trip researching how to run big record shops, ahead of opening the Marble Arch Virgin Records megastore. I was exhausted and had a migraine while travelling near Death Valley and we had to stop the car by some rocks and a Native American Indian appeared out of nowhere and sauntered up and spoke to me. In the short encounter that followed, he gave me the necklace and told me his prophecy about how I would become an Eagle Woman.

It was one of many strange moments of synchronicity that span the breadth of my life and after this encounter I knew I must commit to studying healing practices and that part of this path would necessitate undertaking some kind of training which could serve as a casing for all my intuitive knowledge.

6

My last assignment for Virgin Records was to go to the West Country with a team and open a Virgin Records shop in Bristol in two weeks straight.

People often ask me how I work so hard, seeing as many as fifteen clients in a day, back to back, and I say that in the early Virgin days there were no delineations of time between the working day, rest and having fun. We all worked very hard to get the shop open, cheekily wiring the electrics up to the next-door shop and making our own new shopfront that looked like a church window.

We needed to relax, and I remembered that I had an old boyfriend that lived close by near Bath who might supply us with some relaxing cigarettes. I went to find him and was so tired I fell asleep on his sofa. There was no way of letting my friends know that I was not coming back that night. No landline and obviously no internet. In the morning I got ready to go knowing they would be upset, and he said, "I want to show you something before you go".

He took me on a walk, and we reached a small wood and my heart started racing. We walked to a big house, and I felt I had gone through the cupboard door into Narnia. My friend said, "I knew you'd like it".

I went straight up to an old front door and rang the doorbell. An unusual Russian woman opened the door.

"Do you have anything to rent here?"

"Come in my dear with your friend", she said. "Let's have a sherry."

It turned out her name was Olga. And that she had escaped from the red guards in St. Petersburg, between the wars. Her mother was a lady in waiting, whose gardener at one point was none other than Rasputin. Apparently when the red guards came to search the house, they had grabbed her teddy bear in which her mother's jewellery was hidden. Apparently, she fiercely told them to leave her teddy alone, which they duly did. This gives us a measure of the strength of her character. She was always very fond of me and treated me well, but many people were a little scared of her. She worked for Reuters as an interpreter on Russian radio broadcasts and married Sir Henry Lawrence who owned the house and estate where I rented my cottage and worked for MI5.

Several sherrys later, I had been shown the land which contained a large house for a family who had lived there for a long time and eight flats in the back of the house, also an old chapel that had been turned into a squash court, a beautiful Art Deco swimming pool, a tiny cottage that would become mine, two very old woodman's cottages and an old army hut on the side of the main group of houses. She also showed us the tiny, unusual little cottage and I agreed to rent it and move in that weekend. I managed to get back to Bristol and calm my friends by saying, "Wait til you see what I've found for us this weekend".

I moved in and the cottage was thereon full of my friends from London every weekend, passing time walking in the extraordinary woods and soaking up the magic of the land. Settling there, I found work as part of a team who were setting up the first whole food shop in Bath, Harvest. The idea of the shop was to sell good food in bulk with very little packaging. There was a team of us and we rotated all the jobs and had great fun. We introduced lots of spices and different ways of using stir-fry nuts, seeds and fermented foods to add colour and flavour. We also wanted to sell books on different ways of living, using Eastern philosophies and cook books from around the world. We wanted people to learn about different ways of seeing health beyond the global might of the pharmaceuticals industry. The shop is still going today as I made it into a cooperative and refused to sell it and it is today part of a much larger cooperative called Essential Trading. We had a restaurant which was very popular and I used to make all the baked goods for the shop.

A few years later when I was studying I opened a lunchtime café for all the Virgin Records workers that helped me understand how to run workshops all over the world. These workshops were great fun and included yoga, meditation, treatments, plant medicine, and all sorts of fun in wonderful locations in Africa, Europe and South America.

When I was working with Harvest, I became pregnant. I was still extremely inspired by American first nation culture and put a tipi up in the garden when a lot of people didn't know what a tipi was and experienced what it was like to relate to this extraordinary structure as you lay on the ground and looked up to the sky.

One evening as I was shutting up the shop, I must have been four months pregnant, with my little dog in a basket on my shoulder, a man wanting the last loaf of bread in the window knocked on the door. I put the dog in the basket down to open the door and the dog jumped free and rushed out of the door, straight under a large lorry coming thundering down the hill. The dog was killed instantly and of course the man was very upset. Having already learned not to blame, I reassured the man that it was not his fault. With the dog wrapped in a blanket I drove home to the little cottage on the hill, which Olga had rented to me and which today I am lucky enough to own. During that night I miscarried and made a decision not to tell anybody. I buried the foetus and the dog together under my favourite tree, along with an ankh that I always wore around my neck.

As I was doing this burial ceremony, I had a very strong vision that I must go to South America. A month later, I was there, my feet pressed to the land of that great continent.

While spending time in Colombia, I had a second more specific calling to visit the Kogi indigenous tribe who reside in the Sierra Nevada de Santa Marta mountains, which is surrounded by dense jungle. It came about in a surprising way. My girlfriend and I met an anthropologist in Colombia and he said he had been asked to visit a tribe called the Kogi who had almost no interface at all with the outside world. He liked my beautiful friend who spoke Spanish fluently and all too soon, he invited us to tag along on his adventure. It was quite the journey to get there but as we got closer and closer to where they lived, I could feel in my heart it was going to be both special and extraordinary. And it was.

My time with the Kogi gave me my first awe inspiring life changing awareness of worlds between worlds and what it means to be a shaman. I had the privilege of visiting the Kogi in the mid Seventies. It was and still is the most profound experience of my life. After chewing coca for a while with the Kogi, high above Santa Marta in Colombia where you have to chew coca to withstand the altitude, I entered a ceremony for the men only.

During the ceremony, I experienced becoming an eagle high above the world understanding everything with huge compassion and what is called the Cosmic Joke. Running around in fear we cannot often surrender to the perfection of everything as a journey. Death is only a doorway to an infinite journey of love. It is very much of the shadow or 'wetiko' (the Indigenous word for the shadow) to misuse a plant designed to open the heart and lungs to take us closer to the infinite. However to know love and the infinite we must know the shadow in and out. Through my time with the Kogi, my path as a healer was blessed and there was no turning back.

For six years the unusual cottage near Bath was my getaway from London and I started a rhythm of three or four days in London and the rest at the cottage. There were many kindred spirits living in the other buildings and we had a lot of fun having parties and playing music. It has felt like my spiritual home, then, as it is today, and I see no difference between my body and the body of that land. A piece of land, you see, can also be a shaman. A shaman is a frequency that lives between worlds.

In 1978, I helped Nicholas Saunders launch the first Neal's Yard shop, today a large, respected chain. He had bought a house in Covent Garden with a filthy backyard overrun by rats. After lengthy preparations, Neal's Yard opened with Nicholas living upstairs in a flat and the shop below. I thoroughly enjoyed my time at Neal's Yard, as alongside my job, I was busily making the best of London's booming healing landscape and studying herbal medicine, Homeopathy, Flower Remedies, permaculture, macrobiotic and vegetarian cooking, Shiatsu, massage, Reflexology, magical practices, Aromatherapy and crystal healing. Neal's Yard was so successful we soon had enough money to open Neal's Yard Dairy, Neal's Yard Coffee Shop, Neal's Yard Bakery and then Neal's Yard Remedies.

7

When I turned twenty eight, I began studying 5-Element Acupuncture which is an ancient Taoist technology. It is based on understanding the body mind spirit as a mini expression of the universe.

In 5-Element Acupuncture there are five main essences Fire, Earth, Metal, Water and Wood. The main magic of 5-Element Acupuncture is that it really treats the cause of the cause of the cause so that the person gets better from inside out. We used to put our hands up in class when Professor Worsley was teaching us who had brought this ancient system of medicine to the U.K before the last Cultural Revolution, and ask him 'What do we do about people's diet?' and other questions. He would reply always with great compassion, stick the needles in the right place and they'll come in and tell you they've changed their diet because they have connected to their true self.

I discovered 5-Element Acupuncture when I was married to my first husband. I was always as he said going on about Taoism, Eastern philosophies, connection to nature and the true cause of illness. He came home very excited one day because he had a Chinese secretary who was practising something new called 5-Element Acupuncture that he thought was everything I was excited by. I went for a treatment and I knew this was what I wanted to devote the rest of my life to. I loved every minute of the course and the first time I put a needle in felt strongly I had done this before in another life.

There are twelve meridians that are pathways of energy flowing through the body. These meridians have names that denote a character of an empire. To explain this the heart is 'the Emperor' and the pericardium muscle around the heart is 'the Bodyguard.' The small intestine is 'the Secretary' who sorts everything out. The 3 Heater is like the rest of the people who make the Emperor's life easy every day. These 4 meridians are the four Fire meridians. Perhaps somebody has been in the womb of a very bullied mother and therefore their pericardium meridian (the Bodyguard) is weak. So, they have incarnated as a Fire causative factor. Perhaps their symptom might be insomnia because they never feel safe enough to completely relax.

Clients today, as then, come for a treatment, and I treat their essence which is this weak pericardium, and they find their insomnia goes away because they feel safe and their heart can relax. The names of the Wood meridians are: 'the Planner' (the liver) and 'the Decision maker' (the gallbladder). The Earth meridians: 'the Transport manager' (the spleen) and 'the Rottener and Ripener' (the stomach). The Metal meridians are: 'the Eliminator' (then colon) and 'the Receiver' (the lungs). Lastly, the Water meridians are: 'the Storer of chi' (the kidney) and 'the Distributor of chi' (the bladder).

In tandem, I also studied Traditional Chinese Medicine (TCM) and occasionally use it today. Many TCM practitioners say they practise 5-Element Acupuncture but unless you have been trained in the Worsley manner coming straight from an ancient source you are not really doing pure 5-Element Acupuncture. TCM is a profound medicine and has wonderful results when used by an experienced practitioner.

I have long found 5-Element Acupuncture deeply exciting because I can change the world one person at a time by putting them back into their true essence, connected to Heaven and Earth and all around them in an integrated way. It might take longer than other forms of medicine, but all my clients know that something deep is going on that means they will feel better.

8

The single most important factor for a successful community is for each member of that community to know and understand themselves and their emotions. The only way to do this is to do deep process work around understanding the shamanic knowledge that everything outside us is connected to what is inside us.

Anything that inspires us or irritates us, whether it's an ant biting us, or the annoying way a person brushes their teeth, is an indicator of our own inner state. Of course, we are not always going to enjoy the wind in our hair or cold feet on a winter's night, or sour milk, but our reaction to life outside us and the people that inhabit our world is what counts. Our ability to understand when we are triggered out of an adult state into a child state and our ability to deal with this will govern the harmony around us.

Life is never smooth or the same but instead ever-changing like the weather. Each day brings new challenges, but our ability to understand that we are the creators of our world by truly understanding ourselves can give us immense personal power over our lives. This allows us to be compassionate to others in love, freedom and cooperation and vice versa. Of course, things are always going to be challenging but it's that self-responsibility that will stop unnecessary conflict, drama and stress.

I have watched animals and Indigenous people use the natural fear, flight or fight mechanism for the time when immediate reaction is needed for conflict and danger. After appropriate action they return to a calm state. We on the other hand do not live like Indigenous people with support and abundance all around us from our tribe and our environment. Instead we live much of the time with lack of support and fear all around us, resulting in often feeling over-wired and triggered into a place of stress. It is then very difficult for us to feel calm as the stress is so pervasive and routine and familiar.

9

The shadow is the part of ourselves that we do not see but which directs a lot of how we behave, react to others and feel. It is the part of us that we must try to own and which is often triggered in our relationships with other people. Carl Jung was the first person to name the shadow in therapy. There is the individual shadow and the collective shadow, and unless we own and understand this part of ourselves, we can never really create a community that functions properly.

When a baby is born it has no personal shadow but it has the epigenetic imprints that will be illuminated depending on the child rearing methods of its caretakers. When Jung first started talking about this, for some patients, therapy became much more insightful because the shadow is rather like walking along a path in the woods in the pitch black without a torch.

The shadow can create all sorts of monsters that we are afraid of in our darkness but as soon as we shine a torch the monsters are not monsters at all, they are parts of ourselves with which we can become friends. Try going outside when it is pitch black. The bench at the bottom of your garden may seem like a threatening rock with lots of monsters hiding behind it. However, if you turn on your torch or phone light, it's just a bench. Likewise, we can experience feelings that engulf and overwhelm us, but with the right kind of torch we can bring that feeling to the surface and it no longer causes us such pain.

There have been a plethora of books on positive thinking that disappoint people because they haven't first done valuable inner work. We have to understand our own shadow to understand others and work through our difficulties to a balanced place, not escape or ignore them with addictions and disassociation.

10

In Taoism and in nature, there is a constant interplay of opposites that work together. As a part of nature, this interplay is constantly within us and when we understand this, we will no longer think we are depressed or anxious because we will have tools to negotiate the ups and downs of life. When a parent is perpetually hovering anxiously around their child, this balance tends to be interrupted.

Many of us are constantly trying to be okay and feel ashamed when we feel pensive or quiet in case we affect others. It is so fashionable to always think only of positive things but if we do this we will not understand the depths of our own emotions and nature itself.

Remember what a stormy, windy, moonless night feels like as opposed to a still, Summer's day. They are both important and glorious in their own ways but, especially as British people, we bemoan the stormy, windy, moonless night as though it was some godless event from which we have to escape. The stormy, windy, moonless night is a perfect time to lie in bed and go deep, perhaps into our own grief, and swim through the emotion until we reach the other side, cleansed of some deep imprint.

Without dark times we cannot experience the light times. These opposing forces balance and complement each other to create an interconnected whole. This yin / yang balance is the principle of Taoism.

In the Seventies, so many people found gurus and discovered yoga and meditation and no one was allowed to talk about anything dark or difficult. Misunderstanding the Hindu scriptures they would say, You've got bad karma, man. I found it frustrating at the time but realised at least they had learnt some tools to move some of their stuck emotions out of their bodies and connect to consciousness via meditation.

Spiritual bypass thinking became very popular at the time. A lot of collective shadow got pushed even deeper down into people who refused to ever look at their own shadow or the collective shadow. This created a lack of responsibility towards each other and nature. Spiritual bypass thinking means that in a wish to constantly be positive we overlook the arduous but rewarding journey that it takes to live in harmony with our spirit. We have all been guilty of this as we may use meditation, yoga or other practices to feel better (even if doing so is of course entirely valid as a method of self care). However by doing this we may overlook the deep patterns that come up over and over again inside us and also in our society, thereby not really changing deep patterns.

I have worked with many clients who have not dealt with their personal trauma or done any shadow work on their patterns, and have immersed themselves in the wellness industry, hoping for miracles. They have written an unrealistic wish list for the perfect partner, unaware that they are the person they are looking for. In loving yourself, you make space to love another.

With this list in their hand, they stay in their own, untidy bedroom of the mind, scrolling through their phone, wondering their dream partner is not arriving. If a client is stuck in this daydream scenario, I explain that action is required to get them out of that bed of the mind, to move their energy and for them to begin creating a loving relationship with their true self via effort of movement, both outside and inside.

Similarly, if they have money problems I explain that money is an energy they need to make friends with, and like water, it must flow. It requires action and effort to reflect that energy in their experience. Simply put, it takes work to manifest a new reality, it's not going to be handed to you on a gleaming, quick fix, miraculous plate.

11

A very good development that has happened in the search for spirituality, despite spiritual bypass thinking, is the rise of meditation in the West over the last 50 years, ignited by The Beatles' much publicised trip to the Hindu holy town of Rishikesh set on the banks of the River Ganges in North India in 1968.

Due to large-scale disappointment, particularly from young people, in formal religions that were useful to the previous generations, meditation became an acceptable way of sitting quietly in a sacred space and tuning into the spiritual self, embracing nature and cultivating a feeling of consciousness.

The increased interest in meditation has been an incredibly powerful advance in many lives across the world. In a way it has been the replacement for many who used to go to a place of worship to sit still and tune in. Now the church, synagogue, temple, gurdwara or mosque can be a sitting room, bedroom, spare room or the shade beneath a tree. I would like to see all our places of worship made available for meditation. We need a more common purpose around how to tune in to spirit or consciousness.

Meditation may have formal methods but it does not have rules as such and is really about the sanctity and power of the breath. The breath is the energy of heaven and therefore accessible to all, whoever you are, wherever you are. It is free, needs no buying of equipment and costs not a penny, euro or dime to practice.

A good habit takes nine attempts to become part of our life. Start with five minutes of meditation every day. Either use an app, or simply allow yourself a rhythm of breathing in, to the count of four, pausing, breathing out to the count of six. Start to do this for five minutes per day and increase your meditation by a minute each time.

Meditation is often very difficult for people who find it hard to surrender. Keep persevering as with any practice and you will start to get that wonderful feeling of 'no mind' and being utterly present to what is, without thinking about it.

12

As an energy healer, I have experienced first hand from clients the way that human beings manifest as 'energy'. We are a mass of moving particles in the quantum field. We are also a coded frequency influenced by our epigenetic and life experiences.

Advances in science now explain what ancient peoples have known for millennia. But science poses more questions than it answers and there are still fundamentally mystical things that as human beings we will never have the capacity to understand.

As beings of the earth it is important to maintain humility and curiosity, One should never presume to know everything. Our teachers arrive in surprising packages. If we judge a situation too quickly, we often miss what is being shown to us. We are prone through fear to stick with the familiar and therefore stay with a pattern that stops flow.

Willingness to talk with a stranger or go to a venue we would not normally choose, helps us come out of our comfort zone and from such a place we can learn so many new things. Fear of the unknown stunts growth. Openness and humility often guide us to new perspectives.

Using 5-Element Acupuncture, I work on treating imbalances in my clients' energy fields. The fascinating advances in neuroscience reveal that the mind-body connection is far from esoteric – we really do have a gut brain and a heart brain.

Research in the discipline of neurocardiology has shown us the heart is both a sensory organ and a sophisticated centre for receiving and processing information. The nervous system within the heart, that we call 'the heart brain' enables it to learn, remember and make functional decisions independent of the brain's cerebral cortex. Numerous experiments have demonstrated that signals the heart continuously sends to the brain influence the function of higher brain centres involved in perception, cognition, and emotional processing. The heart also, via electromagnetic field interactions, communicates information to the brain and generates the body's most powerful and most extensive rhythmic electromagnetic field.

We have many words in our language to describe the connection between the gut and the brain and most of us are aware the gastrointestinal tract is sensitive to emotions of anger, anxiety, sadness and elation, that trigger symptoms in the gut.

A troubled intestine can send signals to the brain just as a troubled brain can send signals to the gut. We talk about a 'gut wrenching experience', say 'I cannot stomach that' or 'that experience made me feel sick' and before tests, meetings and decisions will quip, 'I have butterflies in my stomach'.

Stress can create all sorts of problems in the digestive tract like, heartburn, cramps, constipation and loose stools. It is now well-known fact that to be healthy we need a good relationship between our gut brain, heart brain and head brain. I often say to my clients that it is healthier to sit down and eat a packet of crisps slowly and consciously - you would probably not finish that packet of crisps if you were eating it consciously - than it is to eat a 'healthy' salad too quickly in an angry mood. How we eat is as important as what we eat. Food is often used to suppress emotion, to alleviate discomfort emotionally and worse of all to alleviate boredom. And food taken in this way will cause problems.

13

If you want to experience true happiness and freedom, love everyone around you without a desire for it to be returned. Love is an energy and an invisible bank account that you feed into that does not necessarily give you a desired return that you can control. For example, if you are kind to a street seller, they may not necessarily love you back but some stranger later on in the day might offer you their bus seat. This is how the energy of love works, it circulates.

This is what I mean by the quantum field. Indigenous people are very aware of this energy. In the West, we exist in a kind of contractual love space where we give our love with all kinds of unspoken expectations. We attach these conditions to our love without checking with other people that they are in agreement. We often end up disappointed and resentful as a result.

A very simple heart meditation that you can do at any time, even on public transport, is to place your hand on your heart and close your eyes and imagine that the sun, which is out there somewhere even if you can't see it, is pouring light into your heart. In return you are pouring love back out to the world as a warm constant orange light. If you activate the heart like this on a daily basis, it is like lighting a fire in your home and warming your hands on it.

14

It is so important to put healthy boundaries in place. To do this, we need to know ourselves and develop an ability to stay calm and loving when we come into conflict with others. With greater self-awareness we can become more conscious of the energy we are transmitting to others that affects the way they react to us and vice versa. This is especially important around children who are in the 'I' (ego-building) stage and need a calm, solid presence who will not react with volatility but respond appropriately. To maintain boundaries, we also need to be more mindful of negative patterns and habits. All of us globally at this point in history display addictive behaviours around screens, especially smartphones, that can lead us to quite literally, live with our heads down, ignoring one another. Upholding conscious, healthy boundaries around digital habits ensures we respect the sacredness of family and community ceremonies. To counter this, one important ceremony a family or couple can try and uphold is eating together. Cultivating sacred moments that bond us together in a positive way are crucial to the maintenance of healthy behaviours and life enhancing rituals.

15

By all accounts, I had a traumatic time in the womb. My parents were stationed in colonial Malaya, as it was called at the time. My father had a post war job in the army and my mother already had two children. My parents' communication was mainly glued together by partying. They laughed a lot and shared a love of nature but had very little else in common. I was conceived in the previous army post in Klagenfurt, Austria where my mother had had an affair with a skiing instructor (a familiar story in days when very few people divorced). She had no idea who my father was and did not want another child. She tried to abort me with gin and hot baths and jumping off ski slopes and even using a knitting needle to try and break the waters. However, in her own words: I was determined to come.

She had no understanding that the unborn foetus can feel everything and would be horrified to know the trauma I was experiencing in the womb. She was a brave and kind soul that had had a very difficult childhood in colonial India and was really just doing her best. Despite my mother's resistance, I was born in an army hospital a month late with long fingernails and lots of hair. I understand it was a long and arduous birth in extreme heat with no air conditioning. She collapsed as soon as I was born and moved to a bassinet. The air conditioning howled while she was asleep and to this day I dislike the wind. We then went back to our verandah house on the edge of the jungle where I was handed to a very kind Malaysian nanny who, my mother later said 'insisted on sleeping with me'.

16

There is no medicine as effective as movement. Slave to screens - phones, tablets, laptops, TVs, gaming consoles, projectors - we are a people for whom sedentary life is becoming normalised. Never in history has humankind been so inactive and so beached on a slouchy sofa. As we enter the hard sell of the Metaverse I feel it is even more important to keep alive the natural world and our relationship to it. Many people will be attracted by this digital world but I would like to encourage people to remember who we really are before the onslaught of the fourth industrial revolution and the fusion of biology and technology. To remedy this, we need to move. It's hard to believe but these days, movement actually needs to be prescribed like medicine. If we remain dynamic in ourselves, we stay healthy. Stagnant energy attracts darkness. We must also remember that true health is an inside job. So I'm going to repeat here, when you feel depressed, unhappy, anxious, negative – I suggest you move. If it's the middle of the night, switch on the light, sit up and start writing or painting or reading. You could even listen to a positive podcast and the light will come back in. If it's daytime, daily ceremonies, structures, rhythms will help you keep in the flow of life. When things are flowing, stagnation is repelled and darkness cannot settle.

Indigenous people spend a lot of time keeping their yurts, tipis and associated dwellings very clean. They also use incense, chanting, singing, rattling and drumming to keep energy moving and to bring spirit into their environment. I cannot stress this enough: Keeping your environment loved is extremely important to your overall health. I have experienced and learned in my shamanic training that we are not the only frequencies that exist in this space time reality.

We are only using a very small amount of our consciousness and therefore with our five senses we experience very little. Psychics and clairvoyants can see other frequencies like 'spirits', 'ghosts', discarnate bodies and elementals. Other people feel the presence of 'tree spirits' and other beings and some people with a heightened sense of smell can even smell when another frequency is in the room.

When I have a healing treatment, I have frequently experienced a very real sensation of someone else holding my feet, while the healer is very clearly working on or about my head. In the field of energy medicine, this is known as 'phantom hands' where an extra pair of hands can be felt by the patient, suggesting the presence of an extra-dimensional visitor.

Often I have sessions from healers and give sessions myself where other energies can be felt in the room. When this happens, the veils between the worlds are thinner and the healer or client may experience similar sensations. In such moments, rather than question your sanity, try to get your mind out of the way and feel these 'other energies'. If any of them ever scare you, just imagine wrapping white light around your auric field, which is the field surrounding your personal frequency. This light will repel any darkness back to where it came from.

17

When I first visited the Yawanawa indigenous peoples of the Amazon, I was taken into the forest with their oldest shaman who was over a 100 years old and fit as a fiddle. He took a four year old helper with him. He gave me a very large dose of their tobacco snuff. I had the sense of being propelled into another universe where other beings took lifetimes of trauma off me and all the traumas that I had absorbed from my clients. These beings were very benevolent. I sweated and vomited out all of this darkness and shadow.

The old man and his helper washed me and my clothes in the river and wrapped me in banana leaves until both me and my clothes were dry. Afterwards he told me that I would be a tobacco shaman because I had communicated with the tobacco so strongly. He told me he had taken off all of the residual darkness I had absorbed from healing my clients. From that moment on I committed to learning better boundaries around my clients. The tribe gave me several pipes and head-dresses and initiated me as a tobacco shaman.

Most Indigenous tribes call tobacco 'the Mother Plant'. It is very sad that we have reduced this plant to a cigarette with chemicals in it. It is also very sad that a lot of the slave trade from Africa was created to feed the addiction of cigarette smoking, out of the context of ceremony, with no respect for this incredible plant. We even blame lung cancer on tobacco when in reality, it is the way we have commodified and adulterated this plant as we have done with many natural things. In truth we have done this with our own bodies and lost sight of true health, which is a respect for ourselves in balance with the natural world. We are always looking outside of ourselves for a culprit that makes us unwell rather than looking at how we relate to the outside from deep inside ourselves.

18

The reason I talk a lot about child rearing is because it is the foundation of how we protect ourselves from other peoples' energies. Of course we need to experience the edges of life and true emotions to be truly human. However, if we are raised in a way that allows us to develop without judgement by caretakers who are self aware, our emotions are dynamic and do not get stuck in our bodies. This way we do not become hosts of negativity. I could liken our bodies to a pond in nature. If the pond has adequate natural life in it such as newts, frogs, dragonflies and small creatures and a flow of water, the pond does not become stagnant. If it is allowed to become stagnant, too much algae grows that kills the plants and animals and shuts out the sunlight.

19

True health is about understanding that if we are in charge of our own bodies, we are in charge of our own health. In this way we would know that no other person can truly make us ill, make us die, make us angry or make us sad.

They can be instruments of our wish to know ourselves, they can be barometers of being out of balance, but they cannot do anything to us that we have not created or allowed to happen individually or collectively.

Indigenous people know there is no difference to being killed by a microbe or a jaguar, as we are the co-creators, with consciousness, of all that we experience.

We are now in a narrative that the microbe is an illness and the jaguar is an accident. In indigenous thinking, it is all about interconnectedness and taking inspiration from this, we can step out of the triangle of 'victim, persecutor, rescuer' that we so often find ourselves in.

Another version of this is 'problem, reaction, solution'. If we take responsibility for ourselves and understand difficulties inside and out, we no longer think in terms of 'problems' or 'victim thinking'. We then do not react or feel persecuted, and therefore know our way out of the problem and do not need an external rescuer or solution.

If we know ourselves and we know our boundaries then it's really hard to fall back on blaming others. No other person or a special food or anything is going to cure us on its own. The way that we can be dis-ease free is to know ourselves mentally, physically, emotionally and spiritually, and this often involves deep process work around how we came into this world, why we came into this world and who we decided to be in this lifetime.

20

The reason why people keep wanting to reincarnate on this planet and why there is a cosmic battle over it is because it is an extremely beautiful place of many colours and species. On this plane we can inhabit a body in which to be creative. Creativity is at the core of what it means to be a being of this earth. The ability to grow a child inside your body, made by the act of love. Or the fact that we can have a tantric experience where the kundalini rises from the base chakra to the top chakra just by dancing. Both are unique to this planet.

The fact that it is almost impossible to make copies of humans or to separate a human from the soul has always confused other galactic beings. In the religious viewpoint, we are a godly creation and in a sense we are because we are a very beautiful extraordinary piece of creativity. You can clone our bodies, you can clone animals and plants, but you can't clone the consciousness that inhabits them, because we are all 'god' and we are all the creators. Steiner said that he could see around 2020 to 2030 that there was a possibility that we could be disconnected from our soul. If we merge biology and technology, we would become robots. I feel there are enough of us that are unwilling to be separated from our soul. We know we are consciousness having an experience in this space time reality. Only time will tell.

The exciting journey of life is to understand the path we have chosen to undertake, even in scenarios of extreme hardship. Many times we may wish to change our appearance because we feel unacceptable as we are. When my clients feel this way, I suggest, as Indigenous people would do, that they paint themselves, make and wear colourful clothing, dye their hair and experiment via dance and movement expressing many different aspects of gender, age and colour of skin.

I was very taken when I first went to Bali where they literally have a ceremony every day for all aspects of life. I watched a young Balinese person through facial expressions and dance morph before my eyes from boy to girl to boy many times over. It seems to me that we have suppressed this natural desire to dance through these expressions into binary judgements.

In my home, I once did a swap with a very masculine looking gardener for accommodation in return for gardening before we turned it into the kind of community it is evolving into today. After a week I knocked on the door to see how he was. He had transformed this little showman's wagon into a boudoir and met me at the door in full drag. He was playing heavy metal and said he'd never been happier. I was so thrilled the land had given him a place for the full expression of his character.

To maintain balanced emotions, we can look to the ancient Chinese and their understanding of the Tao. Immersed in nature, they understood that with flow comes true living. They conceived 5-Element Acupuncture to keep us all in a balanced flow of emotions.

We incarnate into a body to enjoy emotions; outside of this body we do not experience them, which is why we reincarnate time after time to have this experience. What is happening today is that because so many of us spend so much time on screens, disconnected from nature, our screen time takes over with managing our emotions for us. We can flick from a very sad movie straight into a comedy straight into a horror movie, not realising that our emotions are being pulled like a puppet on a string. When we switch off the screen, we can unsurprisingly feel empty.

One of the best ways I know to maintain this balance is to have regular 5-Element Acupuncture treatments because it allows us to feel our own essence over all the shouting noise that surrounds us. 5-Element Acupuncture views each person as a mini-universe of fire, earth, metal, water and wood and, just as in nature, if those elements are balanced we would not go to extremes. The extreme of low fire is defensive criticism or someone who cannot stop laughing about everything as opposed to a serene and gentle laughter of the Buddha or a small child.

Earth is the true compassion of the mother; always there to sustain you and catch you, to give you water, warmth and food – as opposed to an earth out of balance, where only worry and not being present is the predominant feeling. True metal offers genuine connection to consciousness and all that is out there in the universes, knowing that we are uniquely special but all connected. A metal out of balance feels empty, barren and unseen.

A healthy water flows appropriately singing over the rocks of a mountain filling up with life, or is as deep as a mountain lake or as brave as a wave crashing onto the shore. Inappropriate water is an inflowing, stagnant pond of dark fear with no life in it. Appropriate wood is like the energy of spring, where the snowdrops push up through ice and snow to shoot their little heads up to show us that spring is coming. It's dynamic, creative and unstoppable. Inappropriate wood feels stuck with no agency, does not understand the point of anything and suffers from depression.

21

I have mentioned many ways of healing the body back into equilibrium and balance but I really want to emphasise that this does not mean vacantly sitting in meditation, not really being in your body. Too many people follow other people's narrative for the sake of peace, feeling too frightened to speak up, often adopting cynicism as a way of coping. True calm is purely dynamic like dusk and dawn; you can smell the stillness but within that stillness is so much life. As I write this, we are living at a time where the universal energy is changing so much that the old ways of thinking have no traction. Before people are able to change, they will sometimes hold on to their old ideas like a log in a stormy sea for fear of being drowned forever. I see people all around me holding on to old logs of old ideas, frightened to change while their soul is urging them to do so. When they let go of the log and allow the stormy sea to wash them into shore they can lie back in surrender, saying, 'Thank you, gratitude, love' as the old Hawaiian shamans do, when change is afoot. They can then be washed onto a new shore.

22

It is important to collect what I call a basket of daily practices, depending on your day ahead and how you woke up. If you wake up feeling horrendously bad, which some people do, the best thing to do is haul yourself out of bed and step into a hot shower and then, having washed yourself all over, try really hard to either shout or sing to get the energy moving. Then be really brave and turn the shower to cold for as long as you can bear it. Having dried yourself, get dressed.

If you are running late and have work to do, then your next daily practice may have to be delayed but as soon as you are able, dip into the basket of daily practices and work out which one you're going to do next. Is it a walk outside, is it a Pilates or yoga class, is it meditation, is it making yourself an extraordinarily good green juice or an interesting soup?

Work out how you are going to sort the day out between practices that feed your body, mind, spirit and any other activities you have put in your diary. It could be meeting with friends, looking after your family or watering plants. The important thing is to have a healthy mix of nourishing yourself and the environment around you.

If you've had a day where you have overslept and were on the run with no time to yourself until midnight, it is absolutely necessary to meditate or have a bath for at least half an hour before you go to sleep, away from your phone, computer and other people. If you do this half an hour before you sleep, even if it's two o'clock in the morning and you really need your sleep, this valuable time will make sure your sleep is of a much better quality. There are so many ways you can meet people, even in times of very low income, using your imagination. You can even offer to walk a neighbour's dog.

Each week I encourage my clients to make some kind of loose structure for everyday that will add rhythm to your life and every month do something special with friends. If you have a limited budget, a picnic in the park can be a really fun time. If you have no money to spare at all, you could plan a walk with a friend.

If you feel desperately lonely, you can always find a neighbour that you could help or seek out a volunteering opportunity with a charity, such as a food bank. All you have to do is make the first step of walking out of the building you live in and doing a little bit of research on what charities you can help or what groups you can join out in nature.

23

The lives of our ancestors are literally encoded into our DNA. We carry past life within us in this way. The emerging science of epigenetics is proving that everything from trauma to our behavioural habits are impacting on the expression of our genes. In an immediate sense, the relational experiences of early childhood create a linked series of transferences to the world that defines the filter through which we view all of our experience and relationships. This combines with our epigenetic inheritance to lead us to project our own internal narratives onto other individuals and constellations of people. So if I take myself as an example, I have an epigenetic guilt from my mother's side about a male sibling. Her brother was likely born on the Autism spectrum. This was unrecognised by her parents and their

Indian nanny - they were living in India at the time as part of the colonial British era - was blamed for dropping him on his head. The poor boy was introduced to my mother as a little boy when she was a baby and he apparently tried to attack her. Her parents were typical colonial English parents where children were seen and not heard and they would not have understood sibling insecurity. The boy was quickly dispatched from India to stay with a vicar and she hardly saw him again. She felt sadness and guilt and wanted to have a large family where all her children were happy. Unfortunately we did not get on and I based my life around my mother's wishes that my absolute priority would be the happiness of my younger brother to the detriment of myself. This has led me to often taking on younger brothers and having no boundaries with them, and finding it very difficult to know what my boundaries even are. It has been a lifetime's journey and my younger brother figures have been my greatest teachers. Very tragically my younger brother died at forty and it has taken a lot of inner work to forgive myself for 'allowing him to die'. So what can we do about these imprints? A starting point is to map your transferences. Many of the 'transferences' we have – templates for relationships we have carried over from early childhood – act on us at an unconscious level. If time and money are sufficient for you, I always recommend engaging with a programme like The Hoffman Process, a week-long workshop that teaches us how to understand and overcome patterns we have inherited from our early carers and parents. It teaches us about transference, giving us many tools to overcome problems in our lives. It is a shamanic experience. If time and money are limited, you can work on your transferences through talking therapy or a process which involves 5-Element Acupuncture, Emotional Reflexology, Cranial Osteopathy, Shamanic work, Transformational breathing and Kundalini Yoga. These modalities will get to the patterns stuck in your fascia and neural networks and dismiss the stories you tell yourself that have kept you trapped.

Every person that you come across every day is a mirror of you, especially your work colleagues, your birth family, your partners and your children. No one can do anything to you; they can only trigger your desire to grow and learn about yourself. We must come out of a blame culture and a culture of otherness if we are to survive what for some may sometimes seem a very dystopian future.

Another form of action you can pursue is that of befriending your triggers. By this I mean learn to recognise things that send you into a negative spiral or make you insecure, angry, sad or hurt. Take a moment to list these and think about what might be behind them in your childhood. Can you trace any of them back to a specific earlier experience in your life? And if so, how does this new awareness shift your understanding?

When you are triggered and feel uncomfortable, remove yourself from your current situation - use an excuse if necessary like going to the bathroom - and head off to breathe and calm yourself back to feeling centred. Then ask yourself how old you are and what trauma you are reliving.

A very important ingredient here is compassion for yourself which in turn becomes compassion for others. When something doesn't feel 'right', the best thing to do, using self-compassion rather than beating oneself up, is take a moment to explore the feelings that have arrived in your body. It could be a feeling of over-tiredness, stomach ache, headache, or even a hurting left toe – the entire body is a map of feelings. Which is why I repeat, process work is the most important way of healing. Even though it is important to understand where we are coming from with a therapist we do have to move the stuck emotion out of our bodies. This wish to be kind to ourselves and understand ourselves and in a way re-parent ourselves gives us the will, love, and compassion to tolerate and be loving to others as they trigger us in our everyday life.

When you are put with people in flat and house shares and work situations with whom you are not aligned, I think the first thing to do is to work out what feelings the people bring up in you, then with that knowledge you can avoid potential points of conflict. Having dealt with your side of the energy field that is set up in any group, you immediately remove half of the problem. People feel energy and so pretending that you are okay rarely works. You absolutely have to work out your true experience of other people around you and shared endeavours and then the other people will feel your genuine attitude to bring love, flow and productivity to the situation. The last thing that you want to do is to fall into somebody else's negative projection of you by being lost in your own feelings without a map.

24

In life, it is always important to apologise and move on if you get into a conflict and allow the other person or persons to be inspired to let go too. Remember they may not have the tools that you have to do this but this must not stop you using all your tools to be the best that you can be.

For example, if you have got on the wrong foot with your children, arrange with each one to do something of their choosing for half a day. When they have your proper attention, apologise for anything you have done in their early life you fear may have hurt them. Make your apology without justification - which is likely to be a way of explaining your behaviour away - and without a wish to be right.

If you are in a disagreement with your partner, do exactly the same without a desire for them to do the same for you. Be the one to come forwards and apologise and diffuse.

One of the trickiest experiences that a human can have is when they enter something called transference and countertransference. It is especially tricky because we have a lens onto the world that includes most difficult perceptions gained from childhood. In other words we can create a very complex situation from a quite simple situation, merely with our perception.

An example of this happened during Covid-19 pandemic when we were literally unable to escape each other and the people we chose to be in lockdown with were likely to carry the imprints of our likely transferences. I personally experienced quite a few tricky moments as I had 16 family members and three children with me. One of the members isn't my younger brother but had all the hallmarks of the relationship that I had with my late younger brother. And conversely, I had all the hallmarks of every authority figure he has had. We managed to create a situation of transference and countertransference that led to him leaving. These situations are often extremely difficult to handle but if you have a map of your own transferences you can understand the counter-transference that can sometimes happen where no one is wrong or right, it's just two people in a moment trying to understand themselves.

Transference is created by trauma. Without trauma we can experience that another person is just feeling angry, sad or uncommunicative and feel emotionally, physically and mentally untouched by it. If our very early experience of our caretakers was confusing with inconsistent behaviour from them we have no intellectual understanding at an early age that we have done nothing 'wrong'. A pattern is created and as we grow up and enter adulthood we act out these early traumas with people around us, still confused as to why we feel so young and out of control.

If our caretakers have been traumatised themselves they can inflict on the child a lot of very childish and negative emotions. In other words the experience of the child is very dramatic and literally creates an energetic wound in the field of the person's energy. This goes on to repeat itself energetically with close friends and lovers, people at work or at school in a very confusing way. The wound is literally like a scratch on an old fashioned compact disc that the music cannot get beyond. The trauma leaves a scar on the energetic field that we keep playing out. Once you understand what is happening outside of yourself you can understand from an inner knowledge how to create harmony and flow by taking your transference off another person and looking out for the countertransference of the 'other' to you.

25

My two children remain to this day my greatest teachers. The elder one teaches me on a daily level that although it is difficult living with a child that is very different, if you live in a heart space, conflict has no space.

By a heart space I mean a place of no blame and surrender that dissolves the differences that can be quite triggering into impatience or intolerance. People often have children who are extremely different to them and it takes only love for oneself in the form of healthy boundaries and love for them to negotiate the relationship.

The most important thing to know about having children is self knowledge before they arrive. If they have already arrived, just know that they will teach you every day about yourself. I sometimes meet people with a child that is very different to them - say a very academic person with a very creative child - and what I do is teach them to surrender to the reality that this creative child will find a different way to be in this world that does not align with the accolades of academic success.

My eldest daughter's brain works in a very different way to mine and around her I learn to slow down and stay in my heart and within that love, I find she shows me her best side. My youngest daughter, however, is literally the opposite. I am sometimes so overwhelmed by the quickness of her brain that I feel unable to be heard by her. In this case I learn to nurture myself and know myself and ask for no reassurance from her about any of my ideas and concepts. If I allow myself to truly listen to her, her ideas and criticisms are extremely valid and often rein me in from more extreme behaviour.

So, flanked by my two children I often want to scream 'hurry up' to one and 'slow down' to the other. Through finding my own inner compass I do not try to change either of them and in this approach, harmony prevails.

26

I truly believe that if we could really understand what babies and children need, our whole world would change. It is the most crucially important time of our lives, and I don't think that society truly supports the way that children should be cared for to become healthy adults. Children also deserve to be birthed from a relationship where the two parties are in alignment. I call this relationship The Sacred Relationship. In my life I have manifested surprise pregnancies, with no proper conversation with the fathers about how we would raise the child before getting pregnant. I have also had five miscarriages. These pregnancies and the way I have been a mother, without a traditional setup around me, have been my greatest teachers. However, if a child can be born of a sacred relationship, it is altogether, obviously much better for the child.

27

For many, a lifetime of co-dependence sets us up for unhappiness. Monogamy doesn't suit all of us and many people are trapped in unsatisfying relationships. There are practical challenges to long term relationships - women reaching the menopause as men reach their mid-life crisis is the best example. This explains why so many people opt for divorce. But alternatives to the standard approach aren't easy either - polyamory can cause as many problems as an unhappy marriage, particularly when our codependent tendencies and ingrained unhealthy attachment behaviours haven't been worked through. For single people, too, so much of the apparatus around love and sex - take the impersonal swiping of Tinder - creates unhappiness. So what's the alternative? There is so much we can learn from Indigenous people about how to love one another. From their inspiration, I believe it is possible to create sacred relationships by incorporating Indigenous approaches to love and sex into the way we live. There are two key ways to do this, through ceremony and listening.

Relationships are at the heart of all that is meaningful. Yet the roots of so many of our problems as human beings are inherent in the way we live, love and bond with one another. In the western world, the way we relate to our sexual and romantic partners is contaminated by ideas of ownership, control and the romantic but unhelpful idea that within each of us is a void that the perfect 'other' can fill.

The 'other' doesn't always take the form of a partner, of course – it may be, at different times, located in a child, or a cause, a career, or a home. But the most common of these manifestations is that we displace our own happiness, projecting all of our unmet desires and unrealised expectations onto a partner, or a longed-for romantic other.

Rather than leading to fulfilment, this way of approaching relationships leaves us feeling lonely, dissatisfied and confused by what went wrong. Loneliness is the number one problem I see in my treatment room – it is an endemic in big cities like London, where many people feel extremely disconnected from each other, their environment, the land and the wider community. Many people I meet are also lonely within relationships where there is little listening and scarce presence.

We are so geared to finding 'the one' that we forget about the 'ones' that are around us, who are made of families, the villages and tribes that we have lost since the industrial revolution took hold of all our lives. We now have the digital revolution, keeping us connected but even more lonely in our bodies.

So many of us often don't know where to start to find our tribe and as the internet is largely our communication tool then use it to start a local platform of connectedness based around alignment of shared values.

An allotment, for example, is a good place to share as are open air activities like shared walks, exercise and yoga. So many of our ways of reaching out have been dominated by hooking up sexually but I don't believe this is a very good item as a first thing to eat on the menu. I think it should take its place as a coffee or a piece of fruit at the end of a good meal. So many dating sites are dominated by hooking up culture and as a result of talking to hundreds of clients I am convinced that most people are looking for friendship, shared values, laughter and true intimacy, not a one night stand. These fleeting moments can feel like momentary addictions and in the end heavy with emptiness.

In the time I have spent visiting Indigenous tribes, I have observed again and again that this tendency to view romantic love as the solution to the 'missing part' of ourselves isn't an intrinsically human trait. It is symptomatic of a culture where everything is viewed through the prism of possession. Through this filter, relationships become transactional – you do this for me, I do this for you, while spontaneity and freedom fall by the wayside.

By observing the way tribal people express sexuality, and the ways in which they form and re-form sexual and emotional relationships, I have noticed some key principles that I believe can teach us so much. By adopting some of their behaviours around ceremony and ritual within relationships and by taking pains to communicate and listen to one another more effectively using their methods, I know it is possible to improve our relationships, to live a happier, more satisfying life, free from the guilt and shame we have come to associate with sex.

28

Our romantic relationships show us, at a glance, the essence of the way we relate to everyone and everything else around us. They are a gift in that way – a condensing of who we are. By deciding to take a look at our relationships and open our minds to questioning our approach, we give ourselves the opportunity to press pause and think about the patterns of relating that we are drawn to. When you do this, it's easier to spot the ways in which many of your habits of thought and behaviour within relationships may be working against you. Our relationships are the place where our tendencies towards codependency are most concentrated and obvious to observe, it is worth considering what your unique habits are.

For most of us, there are two common manifestations around which our codependent tendencies arrange themselves. The first is: I'm OK if you're OK. We often mistake this for empathic attunement, a measure of our care for the other. We feel their pain as if it were our own. Our muddle about this stems from childhood. So much of our understanding of what it means to be loved echoes back to childhood and parents who were overly emotionally merged with us, regarding you, their child, as an extension of themselves. Under the suffocating hold of this kind of controlling love, it is easy for both partners to lose sight of themselves. Imposing boundaries and limits may feel wrong or selfish. And conflict within the relationship can feel profoundly frightening.

You may have had a very controlling, unemotional parent from whom you experienced disapproval at the expression of discomfort and have learnt to suppress your own emotions to win another's love.

Babies and small children are hard-wired to get the attention they need to survive and learn quickly in infancy the best methods to do this at the expense of their true selves. Dissociation and splitting off from how we feel has its roots in these early years. Most of us have been left to cry and experienced disapproval at our expression of emotion and try within the love relationship to find the loving parent that we never had.

Deep inside we know our continuum knowledge knows that we should be held close, safe and protected in these early years. If we haven't received this, we feel a large hole in our being. We have been promised by society that this hole is going to be filled by another human and that this will ensure we feel safe and loved for the rest of our lives. When this doesn't happen, the discomfort is enormous and we often turn to addictions to ease the pain.

The second is: You meet my needs so I love you. Many people who relate in this way won't recognise this description because they are driven by a damaged ego and unable to understand that other peoples' needs exist in a truly meaningful way. Such people may be intensely emotionally needy, requiring reassurance, and proof of closeness all the time. They can seem intensely loving, so long as their beloved 'other' doesn't express needs at odds with their own, or contradict their view of things, or the relationship. This love-type often pairs up with an 'I'm OK if you're OK' type who is willing to go the extra mile to deliver what they expect.

29

High-drama relationships can be exciting, addictive and deliriously compelling. They keep you on the edge of your seat and the adrenaline and dopamine rollercoaster of a high-conflict, high-stakes break-up then make-up relationships can impact on our brains in much the same way as drug addiction or gambling does. The chemical cocktail they inspire in our neurotransmitters is identical. High-drama relationships where you keep coming back for more are inherently co-dependent – both parties are getting something out of the emotional turmoil, caught in re-enacting each others' transferences. These patterns likely hark back to family experiences where drama, abandonment and intense, symbiotic love wax and wane over and over. On the flipside, at the other end of the spectrum are people who have such profound mistrust in other people and who are so cut-off emotionally, that they isolate themselves and prefer to live without relationships, excluding even loving friendships.

This is different to the person that chooses to live as a single person, who has friends and occasional sexual relationships. Those who live as an island may be in denial of the connectedness that is inherently human, the need we all have for healthy connections, for communication and shared experience. In the course of my life, I have at times found myself falling into codependency.

In my early life, I experienced a lot of traumatic disruption to my early care-givers, my Malaysian nanny and the wonderful Nigerian people who looked after me until I was five. Having these nurturing bonds broken when my family moved back to cold, grey England is something I never really recovered from. And I had some traumatic sexual experiences as a child and teenager, which left me in a place where I found it hard to trust other people.

I have been married twice, and while neither were conventional, I found familiar patterns appearing in both dynamics. I have had two children with two different fathers and again familiar dynamics appeared.

Interestingly, with none of these men did I feel that they would be willing to enter a sacred relationship with me, preferring to stay in the safety net of their own patterns. I am still today friends with both of them and spend time with them and our children and I endeavour to circumnavigate with humour the transferences I feel from them and our patterns. Most of the time I manage this by practising self-awareness and trying hard not to fall into the setups of my own imprints. If I fail, rather than blame them I use the conflict as an opportunity to learn. This may sometimes involve leaving the room and screaming into a pillow as a way of coming back to centre.

The truth is that the people with whom we work, with whom we have children and to whom we live next door are always our greatest teachers because we can't run away from them. Conflict is the edge that we rub-up against in order to heal and the place where we learn about our own shadow in order to be in a more evolved, self-aware, happier place.

People often imagine happiness is always being calm and centred and joyful - this is not true - happiness is when we are living life to the full with awareness. Nature herself does not always give us a calm sunny day with a soft breeze; nature gives us hurricanes, floods, cold north winds and crashing waves. We love her for this because we would soon get bored of endless sunny days with a cool breeze as we would not be in any way challenged.

I have not in this lifetime found an 'other' with whom I am intimate who has quite understood the true meaning of a tantric relationship based on the flow that exists between two people that are not in transference.

I feel the reason for this is that when I was younger it was very difficult for men and women to have these ideas that I have. I feel there is much more opportunity now for people to achieve a sacred relationship.

However, I have experienced extraordinary flow when dancing or cooking or walking with my very close friends. These experiences can be so satisfying and sensual, without the urgency of my eggs longing for sperm. We do not have to search for an ejaculation / orgasm based intimacy with another, all we need to feel inside ourselves is a true love for our own person and our own body. Fulfilment comes when we are willing to share this love appropriately, without co-dependency or need of any kind.

30

Sexuality and spirituality were not thought of as separate until well into the first millennium of the common era when denial of the body became the popular theology of the day. Now, we are beginning to remember the spiritual dimension of sexuality and are beginning to understand that our lower physical urges and our higher spiritual yearnings can connect.

If I could define spiritual sex, it is a sexual energy that goes beyond physical sensations of genital pleasure - it is not limited to genital stimulation and the release of tension from a quick and simple orgasm.

The essence of spiritual sex is extraordinary inspiration, enhanced awareness and a sense of merging with the life-force in you, the other, nature and all life. Therefore it is possible to feel a sense of connection through dancing, meditating or creating with another or others. You can experience the connection of the life force flowing between your base and heart chakra and your third eye, pineal gland. What follows is a real connection between the earth and the universe.

31

There is a whole story around the longing of the egg and the sperm to create a being which is often confused with true love. There has been a lot of research around the different energy fields and pheromones that attract others at the time of ovulation. The disappointment some couples experience when their relationship feels radically different after the birth of a child and the mother is focused on breastfeeding, can quickly lead to doubts in one or both partners as to whether the couple has fallen out of love or lost the originating basis for the couple coming together. The way around this feeling, as I've seen in so many communities of Indigenous peoples, is to build a tribe around the raising of a baby. In the village, a couple finds support and maintains their pre-parent bond and connection too, rather than in the solitude of first time child-raising and its unknowns, reconfiguring the couple relationship as a family dynamic.

32

Conventional, long term monogamy, as a concept, is generally speaking doomed to fail. In the UK, 42% of marriages end in divorce and around one in five people admit to having had an affair while one in three has thought about it.

Our biology and disposition towards change and novelty are at odds with monogamy. *Sex at Dawn: The Prehistoric Origins of Modern Sexuality* is a book about the evolution of human mating systems by Christopher Ryan and Cacilda Jethá uses a mixture of evolutionary biology, neuroscience, anthropology and primatology to argue this persuasively. Humans are similar to bonobo monkeys in many ways with regard to our sexual behaviour, and there is little to suggest that humans are mentally or physically suited to having one life partner.

The contrast between the way indigenous people manage relationships and sex compared to us certainly suggests that our way of doing things is not a consequence of human nature. When I first visited the Yawanawa tribe of Brazil, I saw women and men with multiple partners. The head shaman who lived to well over a hundred years had many wives. The one he spent most time with, according to his other wives was in the spirit world, no longer in her body.

I found they all lived together in yurts, tipis, longhouses and other shelters. They sleep together in small or large families. They would never sleep away from their young children or babies. But neither women nor men feel obliged to be sexually faithful in our sense of the word, to one another.

The Maasai women of Kenya would live in a clan with perhaps three brothers feeling very supported by all the men. These women are not interested in owning a man but feel supported by the clan and are secure in themselves. They accept that both men and women feel desire and excitement and may have special heart connections to multiple partners. They are connected enough to themselves to know love changes shape and has many colours. I have experienced these different attitudes to multiple partners as a beautiful thing in many tribes.

Also, for them, sex itself happens in the forest, but not in the tribal dwellings. Couples go out into the forest to have sex, but they do not display sexual behaviour in public, only affectionate familial cuddling. This makes sense because sexual touching in public is possessive – it's a behaviour that tells onlookers: 'this person is mine'. As indigenous people do not regard relationships in this way, there is no need for such a display.

Another tribe, the Piraha who live in the Amazon in Brazil, have no recursion in their language which means that they have no concept of anything outside of the present. Missionaries, anthropologists and visitors who have observed the Piraha have been amazed by their sense of happiness and their absolute loss of any form of possession over each other in regard to relationships, parenting or food.

33

In the developed world, we have muddled up intrinsic attitudes towards sexuality and the societal boundaries that have to be put in place when we're away from the forest in cities. We have mistaken one for the other. In Indigenous tribes I have visited, both men and women have multiple partners. Most tribes have formalised structures around marriage – with men (particularly the alphas) having multiple wives. In some instances, women had more than one husband, and informal sex is universally common.

Gay relationships (both male and female) were incorporated into tribal life too. The most remarkable thing about all this, from our western perspective, is that jealousy, within these setups, was simply nowhere to be seen.

For example, when I have talked to the six wives of my very good friend, the Samburu Elder James Lekalaille, they are very happy to live together with each other and the wives of James's brothers and his mother, supporting each other with their children and everyday lives.

Talking to indigenous women, they often giggle about our obsession with owning each other as they know desire is fleeting like the seasons and that the welfare of their children is paramount.

What really matters to them is the flowing energy of the tribe and the close bonds they form within it and showing the child how to go from the 'I' state to the 'we' state with ceremony and Love. Unfortunately we are often stuck in a child state and form bonds from a childlike place, 'acting out' on each other. The adults know that they are all important and will not be abandoned at any point. They do not compare themselves to each other and they love all the children equally.

34

The way we confine sexuality, living by a series of restrictive rules, is symptomatic of the way we control and compartmentalise everything else. Rather than understanding sexual energy as a powerful life force within us that can find expression in a number of ways, we confine it. We are missing a trick by doing this.

Indigenous people, in contrast, have a range of ways of expressing the kundalini energy within us. One of these is through music-making and ecstatic dance – a shared, group expression of sexual energy, where people fall to the ground, experiencing full body orgasms. The photographer Mirella Ricciardi took powerful photographs documenting this and it is a spectacle I've witnessed with the African and South American tribes when I've stayed with them. Because there are a range of ways to express sexual energy, and because indigenous peoples do not carry the guilt and shame around sex that we do, sexual energy is more present, more joyful.

In contrast, there is a dissociative energy in co-dependent coupling that can make sex feel urgent and disconnected: this is the manifestation of Wetiko, the negative energy we all carry within ourselves. Wetiko is the First Nation word for the shadow that we all carry inside us and is there in the grasping energy we feel when we crave another person in the same way we crave a cigarette, or a new pair of shoes.

It is also there when we are absent with our partner. It is cruel to be with anyone and wish to be somewhere else, at an energetic level. It becomes important to ask yourself why it is you're feeling a desire to be intimate with another person outside of your relationship. Is it possible that rather than an expression of your innate sexual curiosity, and a desire to connect with another person, your feeling is a manifestation of a Wetiko-tainted craving for more, for possession of an 'other'?

We all need to be honest with ourselves and each other about our desires.

There is no 'right' set of rules to live by when it comes to sexuality. Some people feel able to be intimate with many different people, whilst other people much prefer to have one lover. It all depends on our intention. We have been conditioned to have a lot of shame around our desires and many of us are confused.

35

The free expression of sexuality with multiple partners, as practised by Indigenous peoples, is hard to replicate in the society we inhabit. This is because our conditioning is so powerful and the roots of co-dependence so deeply embedded within our collective psyche, that many people experimenting with open relationships end up stoking jealousy, compromising their own wishes, or splitting up, often with the end result of swapping the old monogamous relationship for a new one. This will likely cause considerable collateral damage to families.

Open relationships need a few key things to work well – a supportive community network, so that the couple with children are supported by other adults, is a necessity, for starters. In our society it is entirely understandable for a pregnant woman to feel anxious if her husband appears to be attracted to other women. This is an emotion of survival. If she is in the tribe she knows she will be looked after by her father, brother, grandparents. If she is living with one man with no other support her fear may kick in that she will be abandoned and possessiveness and jealousy will naturally invade her psyche.

Feeling shame and guilt, she may compare herself to the 'other' woman and make herself even more miserable. Again, the answer to this is to understand our emotions as well as that the society we have created around us is not very supportive when we feel 'weak' and all our energy is going inwards to make the baby.

Another essential component is a commitment to personal, internal work – with all parties committed to going deep into themselves to look at their transferences and the ways these are likely to play out in their relationships.

This is where the hippies of the Sixties and Seventies came up short: they were looking for a quick fix to enlightenment, but also to sex and relationships, but they hadn't put in any of the deep work and this is why so many of their attempts at communal living failed.

My first husband was very attractive to other women and needed a lot of validation from women admiring him. In the atmosphere of free love he slept with other people as I did. Unfortunately, these others felt used as our bond was very strong and they understandably felt their needs were not met. It was clear that societal rules around the ownership of another due to ideas of worth around property, money and children ruin love. Love should be free from expectation and disappointment.

To achieve this we have to understand our own patterns and transferences. There are a number of ways to set about this deep work: self-study, meditation and therapy that includes process work.

This deep work energetically rids us of the patterns that rise whenever we become intimate with another. Love brings up everything other than itself. It can be terrifying after even a couple of years of blissful love and friendship when suddenly the 'other' doesn't seem to understand us and is acting in weird ways and feels like a stranger. This is when the deep work begins but without a map we get lost and are at risk of either existing in a numb state together or breaking up in a painful way. If we can understand what is going on we can either intelligently and respectfully part ways, or enter a new phase of intimacy.

If true intimacy is ultimately achieved, it is unlikely that we would want to be intimate with someone else but that is not always a rule. Sometimes we can feel so close to someone that an intimacy with another being is totally possible. An atmosphere of true intimacy and honesty has no rules. The thing that really hurts people is when they are lied to and when they feel less than or inadequate through comparison and lack of respect for themselves.

I know several clients that have family situations in which they do not want to break up and have agreed to have an open relationship where they sleep with other people. The most important thing is to sleep with other people outside of your family and friendship group, with someone who also has their own support.

The worst thing is a single person having a secret relationship with a married person who has no intention of leaving their family. Although sometimes this can work, the lack of openness and honesty usually leads to somebody feeling that they are losing out.

Although a furtive affair may look like the solution to a failing sex life in a long marriage, it isn't, as it is usually dishonest. Without honesty our bodies feel drained and disconnected. If either one or both of the couple are able to be intimate with others and remain extremely close and not fall into patterns of comparison, jealousy, ownership and insecurity it can sometimes work for people.

The fact remains that polyamory doesn't work for everyone. It is possible to have a positive and loving monogamous relationship if you set about it in a conscious way. There is much more to indigenous wisdom on relationships and sexuality than polyamory. I believe there are a range of other practical principles and habits we can learn from, many of which have the potential to help us transform our existing relationships, enhancing our capacity for respect, connection and communication. Adopted together, these form the basis for a sacred relationship.

36

The life within us all wants us to flow and grow. Because we are all energy in a human form, we need to move forward. Rigidity and clinging to redundant ways of being, interrupt this flow. When we cling we are like the twig stuck in the mud at the side of the river. By sticking to same-old ways of relating, we sink further into the mud on the side of the bank. This may numb us to an extent, but at a deeper level it is painful and goes against our innate desire to keep moving.

Although clinging is often regarded as the safe option, it is far from secure. This is because nature does not support entropy or stagnation – it mulches it back into itself to create new life. In order to build a relationship that is capable of evolution, and a connection with another person, we need to be flexible and self-knowing enough to allow the other the autonomy and self-expression needed to sustain long-term monogamy.

One of the things I'm most convinced of is that at the heart of our dysfunctional attitude to romantic relationships is the ridiculous level of expectation we attach to them. We expect far too much from our romantic partners and the more insecure and less self-aware we are, the more unrealistic this expectation tends to be.

My first recommendation for anyone wanting to build a more conscious relationship that is better equipped to stand the test of time is to remember that nobody can make us feel anything. They can only trigger us with words or behaviour that sends us back into deep transferences - these are embedded during childhood for the most part, so having them triggered returns us to a child-like state. In order to spot what's going on, our adult self needs to be wise to this and lead us back into balance, soothing the inner child.

Once they are recast in this way, romantic relationships begin to look like incredibly rich playgrounds for self-discovery: the site where these childhood transferences get triggered all the time, bringing them to life over and over.

When we are curious about this, we can wake up, becoming conscious of our reactions, thoughts and behavioural patterns. We can develop self-compassion for these fault lines within ourselves and support our partners to do the same, with kindness, love and humour leading the way. Over time, this awareness will help us grow up.

Self-awareness is the first step. Once you're working towards this, there are two further aspects of indigenous wisdom that will help strengthen an emerging, conscious relationship: ceremony and the art of true listening.

37

Ceremony is at the heart of the Indigenous approach to life. In the civilised world, we have marginalised ceremonies, save for a few key exceptions that have been approved by either organised religion or commodified by capitalism - bank holidays, Black Friday, Christmas Eve and Day, Boxing Day, Good Friday, Easter Sunday, birthdays, St Valentine's Day, New Year's Eve.

We have lost touch with the main focus of what it is to be human. Gathering to celebrate our connectedness and spirituality, not to mention the rhythms of the natural world: the seasons and the changing eco-scape of nature all around us.

It is no coincidence that the same forces have divorced sex from spirituality. We have become overly fixated on the mechanics of the sex act, but have lost sight of all that is subtle, nuanced and playful that sexual expression can encompass. When our aim is to connect at a heart-level to one another, sex can take on profound new meaning. This stands in contrast to sex motivated by the urge to discharge a frantic, grasping craving, or sex as a way to soothe an insecurity within ourselves by binding us to another person.

Introducing ceremony into your sex life may sound strange, and conjure up images of elaborate role play. But what I mean by ceremony in this context is simply creating time to hang out together with no expectation of any end game of orgasm as the pinnacle of intimacy.

What I call 'friction sex' is not the be all and end all of the sexual act. It can be part of the menu but not the whole meal. I think we have forgotten how to love our own bodies and how to relax with another. We expect the other to lead the way, tell us we are incredible and be perfect. We must enter any intimate situation with a relaxed attitude with no agenda over any endgame.

38

Soul staring is an ancient Tantric practice from the Hindu tradition. It's easy for you and your partner to try. Put some relaxing music on and undress. Make sure the room is warm. Sit naked on the bed holding hands, staring left eye to left eye as the music plays. Breathe together in a relaxed rhythm. At this stage, you may cry or giggle, either is perfect as a way to release. You might even feel embarrassed, but just move through it. Or you may feel like getting off the bed and running away, but stay and focus on your breathing.

As you maintain eye contact, use your hands to gently stroke your partner's skin, their arms, their limbs, their face. Stay with the exercise, it can release some deep feelings. You may feel a lot of passion and sexual energy coming up but try to avoid ravaging each other at this point. Those identifying as male may get an erection at this point. This is quite okay, don't worry, just breathe through it and focus on your partner's eye.

This exercise is fantastic for breaking down barriers that have arisen in your perception of each other. Connecting with the soul part of each other helps to move past the projections, transferences and irritations that may have built up.

It is important that this exercise does not end up in dissociative sex. Orgasm may happen spontaneously but this will be from connecting with a person in a true sense without past traumas or fantasies entering the arena.

After a while put your clothes back on and go for a meal or a walk, feeling the easy intimacy that should be now present.

39

The suppression of emotion leads to stagnation and disease, but it can feel painful to admit our true feelings to ourselves as well as difficult to share them. It can be even harder to listen, with an open heart, to a partner telling us how it is for them. When it comes to talking about sex, many people are too frightened to share their honest feelings.

People feel guilty and ashamed they desire other people outside of their relationships. Mothers in relationships may feel guilty when they're breastfeeding and don't want to have sex with their partner. Women in heterosexual relationships may feel guilty and ashamed that the kind of sex favoured by their partner - minimal foreplay and penetration - isn't appealing or satisfying to them. Men, likewise, often feel guilty and ashamed that they use pornography, or long for a partner to have a sex drive that matches their own. A way to break down our shame and fear of expressing our needs is with a practice I call Talking stick.

Talking Stick is a method used in Indigenous communities to teach listening and to allow people to feel heard. All you need is a stick - you can find one on a walk in the woods. Then you sit down and consciously work with it.

It is used in conflict resolution, but it is also useful for those in long term relationships. Each person at the meeting gets a chance to hold the stick and while doing so, they can speak their truth, with the other partner listening.

The non-talking partner is not allowed to interrupt, waiting until the talking partner has finished saying their piece. Once finished, the listening partner sums up what the talking partner has said, indicating they have heard and understood. Then it is their turn to talk.

This technique is powerful because often all we need is to feel heard. It can be a hugely powerful exercise as so many of us are conditioned to shut down our true feelings. Repressing our sadness and angry feelings in this way does not make them go away, it just pushes them deeper into our subconscious where they can cause all sorts of problems. Speaking our truth aloud will help us to feel seen and heard by our partner.

In this listening exercise it is very important that neither person justifies, rescues or walks away from the exercise. All they have to do is listen and feed-back that they have heard what the other person says. It is important to try not to take negative feelings personally, but to strive to be empathic towards the other person's difficulty. From this empathy, bridges are built that can overcome huge misunderstandings and lead if not to a more satisfying more intimate life, certainly to a more respectful friendship.

40

I have noticed that if children feel loved in that important window of time from conception to three years old, they have an innate generosity and understanding that they share the planet with others. Children are hardwired to get the full presence of their caretakers at this time. If they feel shortchanged, they can then externalise their inner needs into outer needs by acting 'in a selfish way'.

My main takeaway from the mistakes I have made around my children's early lives is that a mother should try to set up a support system for herself and her children before having a baby. If you would like, as I did, to have a softer collaborative approach where the child totally trusts you, a large support network is utterly necessary. The fathers helped me when they could when the children were young, but neither were in a position to really support me. I had an excellent nanny but no family close by and my way of life outside of the normal nuclear set-up meant that I had to search for like-minded people and learn as I went along.

If you interviewed both of my children they would tell you they had a very colourful childhood all over the world, surrounded by many interesting people and a very inspiring education. Their childhood was peppered with many memorable ceremonies and unusual schooling, but both of them in their adult life still feel anxious that at any minute they are going to be abandoned.

I was very present when I was with my children, but it was hard for them when I disappeared for a day's work and was unavailable. Indigenous children are never far away from their primary care takers and therefore feel secure knowing that the people they love are accessible if needed.

As parents we will never get it completely right but one thing I know, especially watching my eldest daughter's children, is that I definitely healed many ancestral epigenetic imprints as my grandchildren are able to say how they feel and be heard.

Please don't imagine for a second I have all the answers for a perfect parenting experience, this is not what I am advocating, I just want to give you hope that looking at parenthood differently and building a support network around your baby can offer enormous benefits.

41

One of the most beautiful, inclusive examples of shared endeavour I've ever seen when I was visiting the Yawanawa tribe. I was invited on a fishing trip that started with a trip into the forest to collect a particular kind of root. As I do not speak their language, nothing was explained to me, I just had to observe and understand. The root was put into a hole that they dug and lined with clay. They then poured water on the root and stamped on it until it was made a liquid. We all had a good stamp on the root which was fun. They then put this liquid into a homemade wooden bucket.

The entire village, men, women, children and babies, then headed down to the river. The strongest men went into the middle of the river where the river was strong, with some of the strongest women. The rest of the men and the women were on the edge of the river with small sharp knives, while the children gathered in one place. They were all singing a local song. The Chief then poured the liquid we had collected into the river and to my astonishment, the fish started jumping out of the water. I was later told the substance was poisonous to the fish so they would jump out for air.

With the singing and the fish jumping, an extraordinarily choreographed dance occurred between everyone. The huge fish were caught by the people in the middle and thrown to the women on the side who expertly beheaded and gutted the fish. The small fish were thrown to the children who ran down the river and threw them back in and the medium fish were dealt with by the younger men and women and the teenagers.

The cleaned fish were put in one bucket, the entrails and the heads in another and the entire operation was a seamless piece of theatre. The river returned to normal and we sang our way home with our plentiful catch. Arriving at the village, lines were strung up between trees and the fish were hung up to dry. They made a big fire and created a delicious stew of the remaining fish and we had a wonderful feast late into the night with singing and dancing. What I observed in this entire ceremony was that everyone was included, no one was better than another, and there was a complete lack of competition, insecurity, and unfairness.

42

When I was pregnant with my first child I miscarried her twin at about four months and it was a wake up call to get serious about what was going to happen ahead as I felt such loss about losing the twin.

I then had a long and complicated birth but managed to push her out without any drugs thanks to the extraordinary guidance of a very powerful obstetrician called Dr Yehudi Gordon who went on to open London's then foremost natural birth clinic at the St. John and Elizabeth Hospital.

Through his guidance, I realised that birth is the most extraordinary surrender that a woman can go through. This initiation ceremony for women has been so attacked by a medical opinion around the more important saving of a life than the quality of how a child comes into the world. When you are in fear, surrender is extremely difficult. I'm not saying that we should allow our children to die, but if the atmosphere around the birth was always one of surrender, joy and possibility I think many births would be very different.

Going on to childcare, nurseries and primary school, I know it's difficult in today's society not to have the help of these institutions. However fundamentally going into these peer groups and set ups, especially at a young age, creates a lot of problems later in life as explained beautifully by Gabor Maté in his book *Hold On To Your Kids*.

Not really understanding about peer groups, I took Jesse to her first playgroup for the best school on the Portobello Road. My eldest daughter was having none of it, she just didn't want to stay. For seven days I would take her, stay there, excuse myself and go out. And she just screamed and cried. Feeling a hopeless mess, on the seventh day, wondering what on earth I was going to do, I felt that I failed her and myself that she did not want to be away from me, despite happily playing with other people at home. I felt her tug on my arm as I was lost in thought on the Portobello Road going home with her. I crouched down at her height and asked, "What is it darling?", and she stared at me with her very strong blue eyes and replied, "Mamma I don't ever want to ever, ever, ever go to school, school is not good". I let out a deep sigh and said, "Oh dear, everyone goes to school darling" and she stared back at me and said, "Not me, mamma, not me."

We walked to my favourite bookshop and I stared at the shelves hoping for inspiration; I picked out a book by Alice Miller called *The Drama Of Being A Child*. I read this book and cried. I was very affected by this book as it was the first book that really put me in touch with the pain of my own child and other children who are not heard or considered. I could really understand how trauma is created by careless and cruel child-rearing methods. I really absorbed how compassion and empathy for the child's reliance on the steady love of their caretakers was essential to their wellbeing.

I then researched everything about school, from why we send children to school, to where the concept of school came from. I discovered there was a difference between state schools and private schools. The private schools were an extension of the institutions for the upper classes and aristocrats for the boys to be initiated into representing their class at home and abroad with the skills of diplomacy, hunting, French, fencing. The state schools were conceived by the owners of the factories of the industrial revolution. When the factories first opened, the rural workers who had been used to following the seasons and the harvests and planting did not like following a 9-5 routine away from nature. There was also nowhere for their children to go and be looked after. School was then invented to educate the uneducated rural children to prime them for a 9-5 life. The small farms were then industrialised and the rural workers' connection to nature severed. Later the school of the upper classes was then to some extent made the same as the school for the working classes, except that one was financed by the upper classes and one was financed by the state. The class division was set in stone.

Fundamentally my daughter was right and I was not going to send her to school. I set out on a path of creating a very different way to live. We went to live in the bush in Australia away from the critical eyes of my friends and family. I sold my house on Portobello Road in Notting Hill and put all the money into a beautiful property of ten acres. Two things happened. There was the world-wide property crash of the early Nineties, when interest went to fifteen percent. I had gone away for four months to the U.K, and on my return, I discovered that two sides of the forested property had been cut down for a small new housing estate.

I sold the property at a loss and came back to the U.K, owning nothing, with no inherited money coming to me, patchy accounts and an overdraft of ten thousand pounds. I had a three day tantrum and then realised what a wonderful thing it was to own nothing and what a great way to find out who your friends were. I was walking down the Portobello, when an acquaintance stopped me and said, in a very sharp tone, "I hear it didn't work out for you in Australia."
I said, "It worked out wonderfully, I've learnt so much from my mistakes, I'm thinking of making a few more."
She looked nonplussed, stared at me and walked away. I giggled to myself, because I really meant it. It was a wonderful turning point for me and many gifts came my way after that. When you truly learn something, you get into a kind of flow that brings energy to you, for the next adventure of learning.

43

I passionately believe that nuclear families, particularly in our world of fragmented communities, are not the ideal setting for raising children. When we don't know our neighbours, our grandparents live far away and our friends are so immersed in their own frantic work and childcare routines that we barely see them, we are forced back into the nuclear family. Like the co-dependent marriage the whole family can become fraught with tension. There is a kind of bunker mentality in this family set up where we expect too much of one another, and it breeds an us-against-them disconnection from a broader sense of society and community. Add technology into the mix and what often happens is that families end up living separately-together, locked into their separate screens, and interacting in a purely functional way. Living in a more tribal, connected, and collective way where you have more support has the potential to take so much of the pressure off parents and can be incredibly freeing for the children.

44

In the late Seventies, I ran classes for mothers based around Jean Liedloff's book, *The Continuum Concept*. Liedloff's big idea, based on her time spent with Yequana Amazonian people, where she noticed that babies barely cried, was that young children should be held and carried, and co-sleep with parents until they wish, naturally, for independence.

Along with the interest in attachment parenting, Liedloff's ideas captured the imagination of many new parents. Exhausted and exasperated that many families could not follow Liedoff's advice because they were not in a tribe, I set up classes called How To Raise A Continuum Child In Our Society.

Mothers would arrive and were relieved when I sympathised with them. I explained that of course they couldn't follow Jean Liedloff's advice – they weren't in a tribe. They were attempting to parent like a tribal woman, but in isolation.

We need to parent in a community to hope to offer anything akin to the parenting that Liedloff recommended. The first thing I did with the mothers who arrived for my help in the classes was to take the baby and tell them to go into another room and have time to themselves. They could sleep or read or release their anger and grief at their feelings of failure by bashing a pillow with a cricket bat.

Sometimes if I felt they were lacking joy, I would make them laugh just to get them away from their stuck emotions, because laughter is often the key to change. I have seen many young mothers who also have a demanding job managing their work and a small child so much better when they sleep and breastfeed their child through the night.

Having to get up and prepare bottles or go into another room to attend to the baby, disturbs the mother's rhythm. If she can just pull the baby to her breast and feed the baby in the contented dark of the night with no disruption, they can both go back to sleep more easily. Another incredible bonus to this way of parenting is that I have noticed that when the child is older, he has a trust for his mother and therefore other people that children do not necessarily have for a mother who is constantly trying to separate herself from her baby at night. An understanding partner or family will understand the vital connection between the mother and the baby in the first six months.

45

A baby's neural networks are laid down from conception to three years old and I teach that this period in a child's life is crucial to their further development - this is what Indigenous people principally focus on. I have explained how attachment parenting is vital and how we can actually practically do it in our society. It all comes down to support.

If it's just you alone with three children and a tired 'other', it is very difficult not to resort to sleep training. Having little or no sleep makes people literally lose their minds, but if you have support the baby feels safe in your arms as they pick up all your feelings. If you are very tired you cannot help just wishing they would go to sleep so that you could get some. It is rather like you just wanting a painkiller if you have a very bad headache. With chronic tiredness, the thought of a night nurse taking your baby seems essential.

However, your baby would rather have you than anybody else in those early years and the only way that's going to happen is if you are calm, supported and able to have a nap in the day if the night has been full of feeding, teeth coming through, or some other influence in the night, like a full moon or an unexpected anxiety making you tense.

With this in mind, it is vital that you try to stay as calm and as present as possible in that first year before they are able to walk. This is only possible if you have set up a support system. Whether you are in a male / female relationship or living with someone of your own sex or on your own, it makes no difference – it really does take a whole village to raise a child. We need all the support we can get to be present to our children. The rewards of happy children make up for all the perceived loss of worldly interface and recognition. When you treat children properly in the formative years, they have an innate desire to not cause harm, to be kind to others and live in harmony with themselves and nature.

46

In nuclear families, parents are often busy working just to keep a roof over their family's heads. The children spend large amounts of time in peer groups from a very early age in nurseries and schools or at home with paid help either from their parents' wages or the government. Children have to bond at an early age to someone and if that is someone of their own age, that person is definitely not suitable. They do not have the maturity to make the other feel safe. The opposite happens and gangs and groups appear where the members of the gang or group have to obey the leader who is often a deeply damaged individual. These people go on to become deeply damaged leaders of society and the others do what they say because it's familiar to them. The only way to get out of this is for us to truly see that the co-dependent nuclear family is a very difficult unit in which to raise children unless you have enough money for an army of helpers and even then, it does not quite feel right to pay people to love your children. Children love to be in large groups of mixed ages who are accessible every day. The old-fashioned village in towns and in the countryside provided this pre-World War II. People didn't move around so much for work and life was slower. Now we have a situation where people are stuck in a double bind – they have to work to live and they have to abandon their children to other caretakers to survive.

I find it extraordinary that we still allow our children to be educated in peer groups, with subjects taught as separate entities, so that maths, cooking, English and football are like separate islands. I believe that all these subjects can be integrated. For example, children can learn to cook in Spanish, measure and learn maths and understand chemistry by watching what happens when heat is applied in a particular way. When they are playing football they can learn emotional intelligence by working in teams, knowing that every part of the team is important. With this kind of education they can feel satisfied that they did their best, rather than being evaluated in competition to one another all the time.

So often these days the rules and regulations send brilliant teachers into paperwork, rather than encouraging experience. Education has increasingly become a box ticking exercise to pass exams rather than a system that allows individual curiosity and exploration around different subjects. This box ticking exercise has, in my observation, shut down individuality, laying children open to fears around not fitting, not belonging and not being good enough.

If you can't start or find an alternative school, and don't want to homeschool your children, there are a few ways to educate otherwise. You can find just one like-minded parent and club together to find tutors and groups with whom to educate your children. You can follow the national curriculum in a much more interesting way than I believe is available in most schools. If you are successful, I can assure you other parents will join you. I do not recommend that you teach your children personally because you are the parent and need to remain a parent that comforts and guides your children through the stretch of learning something new. Better that the child has one friend that can be aligned emotionally in the tender years of seven to fourteen than a peer group by whom they are bewildered and may draw them away from who they really are.

47

The Western cultural norm of working towards owning land and property has undermined our care-taking nature because it has taken us away from contact with the land to the point where we are happy to spray chemicals like glyphosate on our gardens and food. Many studies have proven glyphosate to be extremely toxic for our bodies.

Allowing agribusiness to flourish so widely has led us to a place where the earth is screaming out for us to stop. We are at a point of peak exploitation, draining natural resources like rapacious parasites. I lived through the Seventies when cheap food appeared in supermarkets and people forgot how to cook 'real food' costing half the price of the supermarket packaged convenience food. People lost contact with what they were eating and became addicted to sugar, preservatives and taste enhancers.

With this, the ceremony of choosing and cooking food fell behind in the race to convenience. People became so addicted to additives and sugar that children would refuse a serving of vegetables. Today people are gradually realising how toxic our food has become and that 'fast food' can be an aggravator towards ill health.

Nature needs a chance to breathe and we have been given a chance to reassess how we treat our planet. If we change our attitude to nature and how we live with each other we will automatically have a more conscious attitude to our environment personally and globally. If we treat ourselves well we will interact in a more healthy way with all life forms.

Even though the vegan movement has made people aware of the factory farming of animals for meat and milk, we often forget that drinking almond milk and eating coconut products or avocados might not necessarily benefit the earth either. The sending of such products to our kitchens involves a lot of water and general exploitation of nature. It takes 6,098 litres of water to create one litre of almond milk. And over 80% of almond milk is grown in California, which has an increasing drought problem.

Healthy eating trends that worship the avocado may ultimately not be sustainable because it takes 320 litres of water to grow each avocado. The entire coconut obsession harms the environment as in the planting of coconut trees, to keep up with demand, many local species have been destroyed, in exactly the same way as the palm oil industry encouraged monoculture and deforestation, the degradation of the soil then requires chemical fertilizers which we all know has tragic consequences for the planer. Oat milk is not particularly favourable to the gut as you are drinking a liquid, glutenous cereal. I personally find it healthier for myself and the planet to drink unpasteurised milk from a local farmer who loves his cows, or have my tea black or herbal.

Wherever possible I aim to buy locally grown food, which is far better for the environment and health. Having been vegetarian for a large part of my life, if you want to eat meat, which does contain many nutrients that our bodies need, we do have an overabundance of venison, which is a very healthy meat.

I do totally understand if people feel they absolutely cannot eat another animal. There is an abundance of nutrients in other foods such as sprouted beans and grains, seaweed and fresh fruits and vegetables that can make up a healthy diet. I find it sad that local farmers who have very happy animals receive threatening destructive emails from avocado eating, almond drinking vegans who live in a city and have no idea what they are talking about. The local farmers often have healthy organic soils, vegetables, pigs, chickens, cows all working in symbiosis with each other. We need to reignite a feeling for nature by working with her, putting our hands in the soil, and realising the kind of connection it takes to grow food. It is beautiful to appreciate the rain, the wind, the sun.

48

A model of small families not really knowing each other, living next to each other, controlled by a central government is the opposite to the tribal model. Before globalization, there were no countries or continents, there were relatively small groups of people who felt a true connection to the land they live on and each other. This is what we've lost.

I feel it would be very positive to understand how we can share land and respect it as a sentient part of our lives. In my own life, experience has taught me this lesson the hard way. The land where I live has a complicated backstory. I was a tenant there for many years, and have had to move away five times, before finally buying it, raising the funds with a collective, in 2003.

With my family and friends, we have built a collection of small homes, as well as a communal living space where we gather. Having to let it go so many times I truly feel the land is not ours, it has welcomed us to care for it. Even though it was tough having to move away so many times I truly understood how to connect with land away from ownership.

In my journeys away from this land I lived all over the world bringing as much beauty as I could to each place. Often without gain in monetary value. In fact I lost all my money on properties several times but gained so much inner wealth. As a result I have a relationship with money now that it is just an energy like water that comes and goes. I have no attachment to it and therefore the quality of my interactions with the material world are so much healthier. I would love to inspire you that this can be yours too if you do the inner work.

One of the biggest obstacles to going from owner to custodian is to let go of the very ingrained ideas around worthiness. We have been brainwashed into thinking that land and homes are to be owned and sold in a legal contract and if we are a custodian that somehow we are worthless.

In our long-fractured history where Indigenous people have been thrown off land, given no rights and left without their land, the idea that we do not own land is very difficult to understand.

My real home is inside me and that with that stability inside me I can attract people and land that are grateful to share without ownership. With this attitude a kind of reciprocity of the spirit of the land and the spirit of the people can overcome the extraordinary patterns of competitiveness and insecurity.

To understand how to be a custodian whether it's in your own back garden, on your terrace, in your local park or on a wild beach in the wilderness, sit, meditate and tune in to the personality of the environment - you cannot use your mind to do this. Enter a feeling space by sitting in the area and tuning in to the energy of it. Obviously at dawn on a May day in a wild English wood the birds will be singing, the new leaves almost popping out every minute and it is easy to be awed by the energy of nature. However, you can tune in to one tired spider plant on your terrace and give it water and love and watch it respond.

Nature loves us to tune in and the best way that I have learnt from indigenous people or in places like India and Bali is to make an offering of some kind that creates a connection. You could build a small pile of stones into a cairn that makes a symbolic gesture to the spirit of the land or watch a bird feed off some seeds you have given them. Feeding a London pigeon doesn't quite feel the same but it's still a real connection if that's the only option available.

49

Ceremony is the glue that connects all life. It is the way that we channel the divine into all that we do. So many of the ceremonies that have survived over hundreds of years have lost their intrinsic meaning through commercialisation. For example, Christmas has always been a ceremony for people living in cold climates to welcome the dying sun back to life, yet somehow we have turned it into a time of anxiety. This anxiety is created for many people through the purchasing of items that cannot be afforded by many, or a way of competing with each other by people who can afford it. We all want to have Christmas because deep in our collective memory there is something ancient about the dark days, the coziness, and the anticipation of being with loved ones. Even if you spend Christmas alone you can tune in to the collective memory by lighting candles, preparing yourself food you enjoy and meditating on the energy of this special time of the year. However, keeping up with our neighbours, driving a long way to see opposite members of the family in a short window of time causes stress. Sometimes over-excited sugar-filled children make the entire few days an ordeal. We have unfortunately made too many of our natural ceremonies into an industry and monetised them. I have noticed all the rites of passage have been taken over by the unnecessary purchasing of things.

50

In my local, organic market, a wonderful couple shines out to me. They live on a houseboat, bicycling the bread they make to the market. I love seeing the smiles on their faces. The woman worked all the way through her pregnancy and shortly returned to work with the baby on her back or her front as though the baby was a complete part of her. This is how I have noticed all African women of all African tribes would be with their children. This woman at the market, like her African sisters, really appears to enjoy being a mother and integrating the child into her life with no drama. She has no pushchairs or cots or plastic contraptions in which to carry the baby. She has no plastic dummies or bottles and puts out a gentle beautiful vibration. She sells the bread in a ceremonial way, with feeling, in the same way that she carries her child. The bread is sourdough bread with artisan milled flour and has gluten in it. Because of the love the bread is made with, none of my gluten intolerant London friends ever suffer from eating it. They are an example that love is a very important ingredient in the ceremony of living.

51

What I have learnt from Indigenous people is that every single aspect of their day is marked by ceremony, as they live in the rhythm of nature. Their entire lives are marked by a gratitude to nature for providing them with warmth, shelter, food and medicine. Here, we often wake up in the morning to a jarring alarm clock and a sense of dread that we are going to have to fit a lot of activities into a very small period of time. We have to make breakfast, get children reading for school and get to our computers or our work on time. We then often spend time at work not even stopping to nourish our bodies or really connect with the people around us, until we come home tired with a short amount of time to do homework with children, make an evening meal, read personal emails, pay bills and watch someone else's creativity with an exhausted head.

52

School age children today have learned to spend a lot of time on screens in a desperate attempt to stay in the right social circles. It used to be a good thing when children said they were bored because they would then become creative and self reliant. I've always felt that the generally bad weather in the British Isles has created a culture of going inward, resulting in much extraordinary music, art and literature of all kinds. I feel concerned that now we are so magnetised to our screens that this enormous well of creativity may dry up. Obviously computers are a very useful tool for creativity but the dopamine addiction has to be managed. If we live naturally we may be able to spend less time around screens. This freedom from screens may mean that we work harder physically, growing our food and caring for our soil.

In this current narrative people have somehow been persuaded that they have no choice or control over how their bodies respond to disease. We need to understand that our overall health is affected by the food we eat, the way we live, the way we measure happiness and the way we communicate. Perhaps then, we could accept the body we have chosen in this lifetime and find a way to live in it healthily. In order to partake of food, herbs and even wild animals that nature provides, it is essential that the soil from which they are eating from or taking nourishment from is balanced. This is the natural Biome and our bodies are our own personal Biome.

If we eat food that we have grown ourselves in healthy soil and eat it with gratitude, it will have a completely different effect on our body to food grown by agri-business that we stuff down between one stressful meeting and another. I would urge you to watch any work of Dr. Masaru Emoto, the Japanese scientist, who has done many experiments with water.

In the experiments he freezes water into snowflakes, which he then observes under high level microscopes. The extraordinarily intricate fractals of the water droplets change into the most beautiful geometric patterns, depending on how you address the water with your intention or language. The fractals also change if you play music to the water. He has proven what many indigenous people already knew: that water holds memory.

The water that we drink, in which we shower and put in our food should be as pure as possible. If you live in a one-bed flat in the middle of a city, along with your spider plant, you can get a Nikken water filter that will change London water into water that feels and tastes and has the same composition as a mountain stream.

If you can't afford it on your own, I would really recommend that you get together with some neighbours to buy a water filter to which you can all have access to for your drinking water. It will change your life. I cannot stress how important the quality of the water you drink is. If you can only afford food that has not been grown in beautiful soil, you can always bless the food and this is scientifically proven by Dr Emoto.

To bless food or water and therefore actually change its fractal composition, centre yourself and then breathe on it these words: This food or water is full of love and can only do me good.

I have shown this experiment so many times to people with kinesiology. If you are still skeptical about this small experiment, get three jars of white rice and add water so it covers the rice (any water will do, tap or bottled).

Place one jar in one room, place another jar in another room, and the third in another. They must be in three separate rooms – for example a bathroom, bedroom and living room. And over a week hurl insults at one jar – like 'I hate you!' or whatever you can think up. Then praise one jar with words like 'you are beautiful, I love you, thank you'. Ignore the third jar completely, walk past it and don't think about it.

In the experiment that I saw by Dr Emoto, the jar that was blessed with thanks and love just fermented beautifully. The jar that had insults hurled at it turned green and black and weird colours. The jar that was ignored rotted.

As we are made of 70% water, I'll leave it to your own imaginations about what happens when we are praised, abused or ignored. When we grow our own food it is very important that our intention to our soil and the plants and the trees and flowers around us is loving.

In my home in Bath, we have toilets that separate urine from faeces. By reusing our own waste with the kitchen waste and with the fallen leaves, branches and weeds, we create more soil. The two toilets we have go into an eco-septic tank. We do not put any bleaches or chemicals in them and the waste is taken away to be used for further composting. It's extremely difficult in a city to achieve this, but even if we live in a high rise, we can go to the effort of finding other people that might share an allotment and you can build a compost heap together. In this way you will feel connected to the soil and the seeds that you plant.

As per the ancient Russian shamanic tradition you can engage with seeds by putting them in your mouth so they take on your energy field before planting. I have tried this myself and the difference is remarkable. Those seeds will become plants that are like medicine for you. If you understand the work of Dr. Emoto this will not seem like a far-fetched idea.

People often moan that organic food is too expensive but actually if you really learn to cook again, put your efforts into the kitchen and if you use the ingredients in the right way, organic food can be very reasonable. Even if we eat meat, we really only need to eat it once a fortnight and there are many cuts of meat that aren't expensive from animals that have been caught in the wild.

Venison or wild birds who have eaten from fresh grass are good to buy as the United Kingdom, like other places, needs to help nature keep these two animals in check. The deer have lost their natural predator, the wolf, and very often destroy trees if there are too many of them. You will always find someone in your area who will deliver venison or pigeons to you. The same goes for eggs and unpasteurised dairy products. I would never encourage anyone to eat meat that is not wild or a dairy that is pasteurised because the pasteurisation process takes out the ingredients that break down the lactose in your body. It also 'deadens' the life force within the milk.

I'm always amazed how long pasteurised non organic milk can last in a fridge. If we're willing to put the effort in, we can really grow quite a lot in plant boxes that we can secure to our window sills with a couple of eyelets and some wire just inside and outside the window. There is nothing more satisfying than looking after plants and watching them respond to your love. If you get together with a few people you can always share and swap all sorts of things that make your life healthier.

53

I used to treat a wonderful primary school teacher that worked in an area of London where half of the children were from Somali families. Before the children started school, she used to go and visit the families. 20-30 years ago the non-Somali families would have a kitchen and a television which the families would congregate around. As the years went by the cooker would go, the kitchen table would go and the families and the children would end up with take away in their own bedroom on their computer with no family time, drifting into gangs as they got older. The Somali families on the other hand were very female-dominated as the fathers were often away working. They would cook all their food and share it all with the families. Impressed by the way the children were fed and mothered, she encouraged the other mothers to come to a get-together with the Somali mothers on a Wednesday evening to remember how to cook and to talk to each other. It was very successful and she noticed the attention span of the non-Somali children went up in class as they felt nourished by the food and the companionship of the women.

54

Another thing that I have learnt from Indigenous people is that it's important to have a good time in life. Having parties, dancing, making food and listening to music is essential and the party preparation such as decorating the house and dressing up is as important as the party itself. Another thing I have learnt is that it's important to play games together. In our culture, you go away from home to play a game but there are many games that everyone from young children to grandparents can play together. There's nothing better than a group of people sitting together playing charades as these are bonding experiences. When many people cook together there isn't such a burden on one person, unlike in a nuclear family where cooking the same meals and always doing the washing up can at times feel soul destroying. If you make something new for a group of people, then someone is bound to think it's marvellous, encouraging you to continue! In larger groups, you can swap recipes and ideas with each other and cooking becomes joyful.

55

The naming ceremony of a child can be very joyful for everybody including for the child, who absolutely understands they are being welcomed to the world. The material gifts and presents for the arrival are totally irrelevant. The welcoming and the party is what the child feels. Babies, animals and plants may not be able to speak, but they feel everything. Most of the ceremonies around this have been monetised into the baby shower and the Christening. If people want to do these ceremonies, it is obviously up to them. Making a circle around the child and every person saying a welcoming sentence to the child is one lovely ceremony. Another one involves writing on a piece of paper wishes for that child to be put in a sealed bottle for the child to open on their 18th birthday. The fun is in making up ideas for your ceremony. As for naming a child, I suggest you feel into several names and when the baby arrives use your intuition to pick the right one. In indigenous societies the elders will get together and discuss names with the mother and father and the rest of the village as they would meditate with the ancestors on the individual path of the child. For example, the West African writer and shaman Malidoma Patrice Somé did not realise that his first name meant 'he who talks to strangers' and that his middle name was given to him by the French missionaries and his last name was the name of his tribe. When he discovered that Malidoma meant 'bridge to the other world' or 'he who talks to strangers', he realised that before his birth, his grandfather knew he would be a bridge between the culture of an African village in Burkina Faso and a 'first world' culture.

56

The ceremony of bedtime for a child who will mostly go to sleep before adults can be done by having a baby in the sling or a pushchair or in the corner of a room. The baby can fall asleep with an adult in another room and then the adult can return with a monitor. In my mind the baby should never be separated from an adult or body of people before they are asleep. Up to a year old, it is easier to get a baby asleep in the sling and the mother can stay in the collective of the group of people. When the baby is a year old the mother can withdraw with the baby if she wishes to do so, but I have always put the child in a pushchair in the corner of the room where they can be with us, but fast asleep. As the child gets older one adult might have to go with the child to a quieter place while the child falls asleep. Whatever you do, it should not be a stressful or difficult time, which people often make it. Using a candle, a bath, suitable music or special songs that the child associates with calming down at the end of the day, creates a ceremony that will stay with the child for the rest of its life.

§
57

When the child first starts to eat at the table with everyone, it's important the child sits alongside adults in a highchair and is included in conversation so the child does not feel left out. Adults should be understanding if the child wants to leave the table early. Between five and seven years old they are more able to sit at the table for longer periods of time. It's important they sit with the adults for mealtimes and not sit separately with fish fingers in front of a cartoon. The most important thing is for them to feel included and enjoy the food you are eating, with special concessions for the food they like.

The most important thing is that they are included in the ceremony of choosing, buying, cooking and eating food with you. My children have always helped me shop for food from organic markets and supermarkets (they enjoyed the trolleys). They enjoy helping prepare food, even if they chop half a tomato and get bored.

Watching the alchemy of cooking in all its parts, from the preparing of the table and laying out the plates, to the lighting of candles and getting the food ready is fun for them. It's also important that they help clear the table even if it's just one plate and put one thing in the dishwasher, this way they are part of the whole ceremony. They will always have a short attention span for most things but they like to copy adults doing what they do, so it's important to try and include them and not shout at them when they don't do it to the same standard as an adult.

58

One of the most important ceremonies that seems to be completely missing in our lives are Initiation Ceremonies for teenagers. Indigenous people are very aware that there must be a ceremony to take a young woman or young man around the ages of thirteen to sixteen through some sort of initiation for them to transition from child-like selfishness of the 'I' and ego into mature experience of the 'we' and community.

The initiations are always done by women for the girls and by men for the boys. Part of the initiation is for the girls to get prepared for motherhood which includes complete surrender of their bodies to open for the child to come into the world, and for the all-consuming breast feeding in those first few years.

The mother needs to feel safe and loved in the certainty that her primary attention is to keep space for her child to grow and evolve. In our culture she often has a partner that has to earn the money whether it's at home or outside of the home, other children to think of and a household to run. This is a lot to manage and often results in her feeling that she does nothing very well, which can be very soul destroying.

So many women are girls still and are not prepared for the surrender of motherhood. For the European female teenager, a ceremony that involves the support and love of women for the individual expression of what it is to be a woman, is necessary. In our culture we seem to have some ideal view of what a woman should look like. This ideal has been based on how we women judge how women should look for men and we can be very harsh to ourselves and other women if this peculiar ideal fed to us by marketing, is not met.

I think we have to be creative and make up different ceremonies in each culture that can allow a woman to accept herself just as she is. She can then go forward into life in a confident way. With the way that social media has gone recently, the absolute opposite is occurring. This is a very important aspect that we, as a society, must address, by bringing it out of the shadows of the manipulations of big tech on vulnerable minds. I would like to encourage young girls to conceive of a ceremony of initiation that would suit them individual to individual. Because the essence of femininity is Yin, the kind of ceremony that I would do would be in a cosy room with candles everywhere and a lot of massage, singing, storytelling and nurturing.

For men, there are initiations that some enlightened men do where young men are taken out into the forest or into the mountains. They camp out under the stars, make fires, learn how to hunt a wild animal, cross freezing rivers, and test their Yang and their strength.

59

Another ceremony that has always been part of being human is the marriage ceremony. What does marriage mean for us today? I believe that love between two people and therefore their children and the people around them can be a beautiful ongoing energetic exchange.

A marriage ceremony sets something in stone for the future, and this is impossible because we are always changing. However, if we choose the words carefully and create a bond of ongoing growth and commitment to that growth, we can create a ritual of great meaning witnessed by many people, as a point in time to go forward from. It is also there to remember when the relationship feels strained in times to come.

My suggestions are that many of the old words of all of the religions are today rather outdated, including particularly the father giving away the daughter to another man. The previous idea of the father giving away his daughter may have been appropriate in other more ancient civilisations but doesn't really translate away from the original context into modern life. I think it is often appropriate that the bride walks into the marriage space accompanied by people that have been in her life like grandmother, mother, best friends, father, sisters, brothers. I think it's important for the bridegroom to do the same as a symbol of going from one life into another, but without losing the great friendships and ties to the life that they have lived up till now.

Many marriage ceremonies are symbolic of cutting off from the past and the woman becoming owned by the husband in another life. This is obviously completely inappropriate for the kind of life we are talking about in this book. So my suggestion for a beautiful marriage day would be that the bride is dressed by all of her friends and family in a beautiful dress in which she feels wonderful. She spends time on her hair and her make up, using flowers to feel beautiful, which every bride in every culture has done.

My Indigenous friends spend a large amount of their day painting themselves and dressing up. I think it is intrinsic to the nature of being human. For millennia we have dressed ourselves in skins and feathers and made beautiful garments out of anything nature gives us. We have created wool and silk garments with beautiful natural dyes forever. I suggest the bridegroom dresses himself in exactly the same way. I have no idea why we have reduced men to a black suit and a tie – how incredibly boring for him. He can really go to town with dressing up and feeling wonderful.

People often ask me to conduct their wedding. When the bride and the groom have appeared flanked by all the courtiers in the marriage place, I tie their hands together with yellow ribbon which I often get the children to help me with. They cut the ribbon into many pieces so each child has a piece to tie round the bride and grooms hands that are clasped together. They can then make up words to make a sacred vow to each other that has nothing to do with owning each other or property but more to do with honesty, not blaming, taking responsibility, shared values, alignment and freedom.

We really have no idea how long relationships may last. Some are literally destined to last the whole of our lifetime and some are not. This does not take away from the intention at the ceremony for each person to be completely present to each other whilst with each other. I think in the vows it's very important to include a wish to remain kind to each other, whatever happens. The two words, kindness and generosity are very important words when it comes to a relationship having any durability. I think it's a great mistake to make marriage legal and can create contractual problems around money. I think whoever has more money than the other is irrelevant.

I know so many couples that have got married, said lots of wonderful things to each other but haven't really talked about how they are going to negotiate difficult times. They don't even have an idea of an emotional toolbox to use to solve arguments. They don't even talk about how aligned they are over their friends or their birth families. Sometimes they haven't even discussed how they'd like to live or even if they like each other's pets.

Of course we're never going to be completely aligned over everything but there has to be a said tolerance of the different aspects of each other's lives. I see so many families argue over things that should have been understood long before they live together or get married. I am sure many people will argue with me over the legal aspect of the bond of love but I have experienced many successful couples who are not married and I have also experienced some kind of deadening of the relationship after the legal contract. However for some people the legal contract is perfect.

Fundamentally I am saying that as women we need to get our ducks in a row and ensure we have support around us that isn't just our partner before we have children. We have to be prepared for the complete surrender that having a child, conception to three years old, entails. As a man, I think we have to understand that just because we may be earning more money than the mother out in the world in the first three years, it does not entitle us to have our socks washed and meals cooked. These old-fashioned roles are not working really in this modern society and a lot of people are ending up in divorce from expecting the marriage to be as stable as that of their grandparents, without being willing to adopt the separated roles that their grandparents had.

60

Feng Shui is profound and complicated and requires a proper Feng Shui practitioner to come to your house. I have studied Feng Shui extensively. Feng is the word for the energy or the chi that flows above the ground, and Shui is the word for the energy that flows below the ground. Properly done, Feng Shui is an analysis of the astrology of the house, the area and the inhabitants. It can have a profound effect on the way you live.

Wherever you have a mess that collects dirt and dust and things you don't really use very much, papers you have not dealt with, and clothes you will never wear again, as you have probably gleaned from the many articles about Marie Kondo in recent years, you have stagnant energy. This stagnant energy collects more stagnant energy and starts to weigh down the flow of your living.

The home is much like your own body. If you eat all the wrong foods and your colon is not working, it's going to make you feel heavy in the head. If the rooms that you are living in are weighed down with unused messy items, you feel stagnant in that room. It is always really valuable to set aside one day or several days depending on the amount of mess, where you are determined to sort through all of the things that you don't really use and find them homes in charity shops or for other people or to the tip.

If you have any doubt about an item, you can put it in another pile to be looked at later. If we're really honest, a lot of stuff around us we don't have a relationship with anymore and it's time to let go. We deserve to be surrounded by objects of beauty.

These objects of beauty and their importance to us change as we change. It's perfectly okay to give them to someone else. I think anyone will tell you that they put half their stuff in storage when they moved house and then wonder what they were doing holding onto all this stuff when they eventually cleared the storage space out.

In terms of the Shui, it's extremely important to have a healthy relationship with the land we live on and in a place as small as the British Isles much of the land has been fought over with, ensuing energetic imprints of anger, violence and grief. There are space clearers and healers that can come and help you clear this damaged land. Even if it doesn't seem obvious, once someone has cleared the land, you can really feel the difference. Land can be crisscrossed with something very similar to acupuncture meridian lines called ley lines. For various reasons these lines suffer from geopathic stress which can affect us. There are various ways to heal this. One is to utilise machines that send out a positive magnetic energy to counteract this stress. The one I use is called a Geomack.

If you read a book about Feng Shui you can work out the best direction for you to sleep and eat in, even if you live in a studio flat. If you don't trust your own instincts there are many practitioners that can help you. It is always good to live with plants because if nothing else, they take in carbon dioxide and give off oxygen and they are important friends to live with.

61

Crystals have gained in popularity recently because people have started to tune in to the fact that they are the oldest form of energy on the planet. Although their frequency is much slower than ours, they contain memory that can help with our frequency. Different crystals have different properties and often if you are in a shop that sells crystals you feel an affinity to one, and that crystal is there to help you.

One of our senses that is extremely important is our sense of smell. It's very important that you surround yourself with scents and perfumes with which you feel aligned both in your body and your home.

Indigenous people collect resin from the forest or make oils from flowers that they use every day in their ceremonies. Every plant and tree has a language and a signature that is conveyed via smell. Of course birds, butterflies, and caterpillars are attracted or repelled by the aroma of their surrounding family of plants and trees.

We don't realise how important our smell is in attraction to each other. Most people may not know that a woman on the pill smells completely different to a man when she comes off the pill or when she is pregnant. He may be attracted to her 'on the pill aroma' and then to both of their consternations find that the attraction has gone down by 50% when she is pregnant. Only a relationship that has been based on more superficial physical or sexual attraction will be upset by this factor.

I have a particular rose oil in my practice. The aroma of rose opens the heart chakra and I have always used rose as I want my healing to be primarily of love. People remember at the end of my sessions that I am channeling an intergalactic divine love through my hands into their pineal gland with the smell of rose and they will often buy my rose oil or my rose creams in order to reconnect to that feeling of divine interconnectedness.

Likewise, there is an upside and a downside to the extraordinary power of our sense of smell. The only way I could remember one of my episodes of abuse was by remembering the smell in the room. By remembering the smell I started to track pictures and feelings that eventually led me to remember. The smell was not pleasant, nor was the incident. I often notice that different smells will appear in peoples houses that have got nothing to do with the house or people, but some sort of message that another presence is nearby. Obviously if that smell seems unpleasant to us it's an indication of an energy that we feel is made up of a different energy to us.

It can also indicate an unhappy trapped energy from stagnation, previous arguments or a different frequency to us.

62

Indigenous people absolutely accepted that the energy of their ancestors is around them all the time as are the energies and spirits of other worlds from other galaxies and other parts of nature. Until relatively recently we have scoffed at this notion but there is growing interest in these worlds that we can't necessarily see or touch with our limited five senses. Ancient peoples understood that rocks and crystals are the oldest form of energy and like water can hold and administer intention and support. Likewise, aromas made from different herbs and flowers hold energy and influence that can affect our mood and sense of balance.

You can start by feeling your way into collecting rocks and stones and pieces of wood from nature and experiencing how they make you feel when they are in your home. They become friends after time. The same can be said for your gardens and your houseplants.

Experiment with the oils and the perfumes that you wear and the incense that you burn. Incense has always been used in all areas of philosophy and religion to clean a space of unwanted negative energies. It is a cleanser. We all like to lie in a bath and be transported to a happier place by the smell of the oil. These simple things can make such a difference to how you enjoy your life. It is not difficult to make your own oils. You can buy a bottle of almond oil and add rose petals or lavender flowers. Or for a stronger smell, rosemary or pine needles.

There is something very satisfying about the creation of a kind of altar with the rocks and the flowers and the essences that you have made from your surrounding environment. It creates a connection that is truly wonderful to experience.

63

I have always had a strong relationship with the notion of a life lived before this one. All Indigenous people have an awareness of this concept. We know from quantum physics that the particle and the observer are not separate and a particle can be in two places at once. It is therefore not too difficult to understand concepts of other lives and other realities.

My first experience of this was a near death experience as a child that I was unable to share with anyone in my family. It's not because they wouldn't have believed me, I just didn't feel that there was a language in my family that would understand what had happened to me. After we returned from Africa I was sent to a very normal British primary school and was extremely unhappy. For a whole term none of the children played with me and I became increasingly withdrawn. The reason that the children were not playing with me was because I had a very extroverted father who would pick me up every day and talk to the headmistress and the teachers. A very influential little girl in my class was very jealous of me because her father had somehow disappeared when she was a child. This is not an unusual thing to happen these days but it was then, in a very white privileged school setting. I didn't want to complain to my family because there was not much room for complaint in a world that had only just recovered from the atrocities of war. We all had to put on a brave face and get on with it.

At the same time as missing the warmth of Africa in every way, I found myself living in a family where a new baby had arrived, without my mother having any help. My parents had also bought a house with a large garden and all the work that entails. I was so unhappy that I had a constant dripping nose, sore throat and could not stop sleeping. My parents took me to the tropical diseases hospital to see if I had picked something up in Africa. In the end the solution was to put me into a hospital to take out my tonsils and adenoids. In those days they didn't encourage much visiting because it might upset the child.

I woke up alone in a separate ward to the main ward because the hospital was so busy with only one other child on life support. I awoke with such a painful throat that I decided my parents had put me into hospital to die. So, I decided to do just that. I remember my soul leaving my body and looking down at this small child in the bed with no regret. There was a feeling surrounding me of unbelievable light and beauty as I floated up a white tunnel. A voice said, 'It is not your time to leave but we are going to send you back with help'.

Suddenly I was back in the bed with an incredible light around me in the shape of a nine-foot angelic presence that has been with me ever since. When I came home I was a very changed child, extremely independent and enormously happy to look after my younger brother who became my best friend. I soaked up the beauty of my environment which was a very large garden, horses, a dog and all of the life of a village. I had a completely new relationship with my parents that I had not had previously. I knew then that we are a soul having a human experience and that everything that we experience is perfect and only for learning in this space time reality.

To all Indigenous people, their ancestors are still with them, as if they are still in this space time reality. I heard from a scholar that the last time in Europe that we had a profound understanding that our ancestors are still with us was when we lived on the commons, before they were taken away from the people. When their parents and grandparents died they would be buried in barrows. The thigh bones and the skull would be kept to be brought out on special occasions. When the people were driven off the common land, several of them took to living in boats on the sea and this is the origin of the flag of pirates of the skull and crossbones. This symbol, of which there are many stories, has turned up in many cultures around the world over millennia.

The way Indigenous African people kept the memory of the ancestors alive was to have an altar in the village dedicated to them. Until recently I had a house in Kenya and the man who managed the house for me when I was away, remembered as a child that his father made offerings to an altar in the village to the ancestors every day, as if the ancestors were still with them.

When the missionaries came, they did away with this superstitious notion and the altars were no longer a part of everyday life. When people die it is very easy to tune in to their frequency immediately after and for several months before their frequency appears to go to another place. For example, as I am writing this, my friend phoned me to say that her father had died the night before and I immediately felt my hair was standing on end and there was a tingling through my body, especially in my knees which was rather peculiar. I knew it was his frequency trying to talk to me so I emptied my mind and entered my heart only and could feel him saying he was sorry he had no time to say goodbye. He had become very ill after a medical treatment and had felt too unwell to phone her. In the night he had fallen out of bed and was found very cold on the floor, dead. His message to her was that he was in a place of beauty only concerned that she was upset that he hadn't said goodbye. It was a very powerful moment and I could see his ancestors behind him, especially his grandmother welcoming him to this place of love. He knew it was the perfect time for him to die.

Even though our loved ones leave a body, their frequency and influence is still all around us. I would encourage everyone to make an altar to their ancestors in the room, house or garden and tune into their assistance and their love on a regular basis with simple offerings of food, fruit, incense and candles. Children especially like doing this as their minds are open and they have not learned to be cynical.

64

Ceremony is hugely important to Indigenous people. It's equally important to the rest of us in the civilised world too. We seek out ceremony in a range of forms: yoga retreats, music festivals, marches and fellowships, as well as conventional religious gatherings and social events such as parties, weddings and wakes. Indigenous life revolves around regular ceremony, to the sun, the moon, the seasons and the weather and to ourselves. You can live in the middle of a city and have ceremonies. We need to understand the importance of ceremony to rebuild our connection to nature and also to each other. Ceremony, whether in the form of a shared meal or a midsummer party, binds us to the people around us. The effort of creating it together is half the fun.

65

When I had my shamanic downloads, I experienced a vision of myself as an eagle. When someone has a shamanic download they go into an altered state achievable either through meditation, the taking of plant medicine or in a near death experience. In this experience they cross what we call lines of place, space and time, giving a complete view of interconnectedness that explains usually impossible concepts to the normal mind. In this altered state I saw that I was able to take a birds-eye view on our way of life. I saw the journey of all people and all life. I'm often asked by clients how they can discover a sense of oneness, a sense of being connected to the living, breathing life force within us and within other people. People often think that I am a special human being and that is not true. Like everyone, I have had many awful things happen to me and have lost my way many times making lots of mistakes. However, even in the darkness I have remembered that it would be ridiculous as I look up at the night sky to think that creation is some random mistake. Nature is so beautiful and interconnected, there has to be some extraordinary divine plan that we are all a part of.

66

Interest in plant medicine has exploded in recent years. Ayahuasca ceremonies are a popular business and ancient rituals have become commercialised. There are tribal retreats marketed to spiritually curious tourists as quick fixes to deep rooted emotional problems. Some are run by shamanic healers with many years of experience, but many are not. There are westernised versions where the psychoactive compound ingredient from the vine DMT is used. Some of these are conducted by experienced shamans, but others may be considerably less so.

The problem with the way Westerners tend to think of plant medicine is that we hope it'll be a shortcut to enlightenment or the healing of trauma. But if we approach plant medicine in this way, it will not work for us – we have to be engaged with the deep process of working through our own unconsciously imprinted transferences for plant medicine to work its magic.

Ayahuasca isn't the only medicine with healing and mind-expanding powers. Each continent has its own native equivalent. In the U.K, ours is mushrooms, and these can be equally as powerful, used in ceremony. LSD and other psychoactive drugs can have a place, if you wish to microdose them but I cannot recommend them otherwise.

There is currently growing academic and scientific research centred on the use of psilocybin as a treatment for depression and addiction. Ibogaine, the active ingredient in the shrub Iboga, can be used for these problems with great results.

The most important thing is that any plant medicine, including tobacco and marijuana, must be taken with great respect and in ceremony with an elder or guide to take you on the journey of ego death. I think that if it is used responsibly, psilocybin could be a part of a valuable initiation ceremony for our younger people to experience going from peer group ego state to the 'we' state of collective responsibility.

The biggest trap for the misuse of plant medicine is using the ingredients of the medicine to get 'out of it' and away from ourselves. We have become so used to using any drugs natural or chemical to do this, that we have forgotten to respect the plants. The plants and the trees that we live amongst have enormous gifts for us. Many of the ways of healing our bodies come from these plants.

Plant medicine has a way when taken properly of reconnecting us with the natural world. If plant medicine is abused it does just the opposite. If we start with tobacco that the indigenous people call the mother plant, we have a long way to go to return ourselves to a respectful relationship with this plant. Indigenous people truly understood the power of nicotine and its ability to calm our emotions and connect us to a higher source.

When the colonials discovered tobacco and its addictive properties if taken out of ceremony, we fuelled further the slave trade from Africa to the

Americas, to feed our voracious appetites. The ridiculous truth is that only the first draw of a cigarette feeds the addiction, the rest could be thrown away, it's that first hit of nicotine that everybody is after. The old ways of taking tobacco was to chew it in a sacred way to release the properties or to take it as the Yawanawa call it 'rape' which is a ceremony blowing tobacco and other herbs up the nose up into the brain, which the Victorians turned into Snuff.

I trained as a tobacco shaman and really understand its unique properties and take it only once a year in ceremony. The tobacco pipe of the first nation Americans was called the peace pipe and was passed around as a peace offering between the tribe and nature. When taken in this way tobacco loosens the tongue and when passed round a tipi it enables someone to sing a song or recite profound poetry that they channel.

The first time I experienced this properly was after a five day ceremony in the south of Brazil. I was up in the mountains having taken no food or water for five days and five nights, with a sweat lodge before and after. Before we had any food, we passed a pipe around the circle of people who had gone up into the mountains on their own piece of land and I found myself singing The Beatles' 'All You Need Is Love' when I was passed the pipe, which amused me as I sang it quite well in a voice I didn't even recognise. I have also taken tobacco soaked in water up the nose with a kind of syringe which was unbelievably powerful with a tribe from Northern Canada. Because nicotine is so addictive, I really believe that of all the plants, it really needs to be treated with the most respect.

Ayahuasca is not addictive and incredibly enlightening but when taken addictively it can start to bring out only your shadow without the light. Originally in South American tribes some young person or a member of the tribe would decide to be an ayahuasca shaman and to do this they would do the 'diet'. They would go into the rainforest for three months to three years and only taking rape and ayahuasca. They would have very little food or water which would be brought to them as they would be in isolation in the forest. In that time they would communicate with the plants and trees and download messages for themselves and for humanity which they would make into a song called 'Ikaros'.

The person would then come back and make a brew of ayahuasca which contains the vine plus other plants. In a ceremony cups of the dark brown liquid are handed to members of the tribe who would want healing for something they were perhaps having trouble with emotionally, physically, mentally or spiritually. And while the person journeys, they would sing the Ikaros and therefore make a direct connection between the healing of the plants and the forest and the person. Taking a watered-down version of a paste smuggled into a city in Europe in someone's sitting room without a shaman is not exactly the same thing. However, if the intention of the people is for the bettering of themselves and the world and a true wish to connect with nature, I don't think the plant would allow itself to find itself in the hands of people without some divine plan.

The same goes for Iboga, an extremely valuable plant for addiction. I feel Iboga is less likely to be brutalised because the Iboga journey is not an easy one. It's a real journey into the shadow to heal people. It is still however a limited resource that must not be abused. The same goes for Peyote, again a limited resource with extraordinary powers.

Mushrooms are very abundant and it's hard to mess them up unless they are grown illegally in the wrong conditions. They are 98% safe to take, as long as the recipient doesn't completely overdo the dose. It is my worry that the pharmaceutical industry wants to copy psilocybin because it will never be the same as the mushroom. I do feel the taking of mushrooms properly could be the saving of our entire world as they are literally the natural internet, their powers are extraordinary on all levels to enlighten us. They can also eat up our rubbish, plastic and oil spills. They are a food and a connector of all life.

Marijuana is a plant that grows in very hot places and has always been used to calm and give strength to those who work and live in these places. CBD oil which I think everyone knows is the plant without the THC which makes you high is an incredibly new and valuable addition to medicine cupboards. Marijuana with THC can be helpful if taken respectfully and can be a guide to seeing the natural world.

The coca leaf is a wonderful leaf when taken properly as the Kogi do. It's hard work to get high off the coca leaf, it needs to be chewed for hours along with a particular sea shell that needs to be crushed to ignite the ingredient in the coca leaf. An entire industry of the white powder called cocaine has slaughtered and maimed people and has given rise in my opinion to a crazy world of 24 hour application. Without cocaine's trend setting in the Eighties, we would not have the incessant working life, stuffing a sandwich in the middle of the day and working through the night. The misuse of the coca leaf might be the worst of anything that I have witnessed in my lifetime.

The poppy plant grows in the high mountains of places like Afghanistan because it is a plant that creates a substance that has been made into heroin. This substance takes away all pain and guides people to the doorway of death. It is a highly dangerous substance to use recreationally and I could never ever condone it being used in this way. It has caused so much pain, misery and death and yet without morphine people would die in agony.

There are lots of designer drugs that I won't go into but the one our young are taking most is ketamine which most people know started out as an elephant tranquilliser. The reason it is attractive to young people is that again it allows people to forget their troubles and feel soothed. The taker of ketamine feels connected to the people they are taking it with, and to other worlds of colour and possibilities but it has two physical downsides. One is that it ravages the body, particularly the bladder, and it closes down the pineal gland by creating crystals over this important gland which we call the third eye. It appears to open the third eye from within which is why people love it. But after too much ingestion of it the pineal gland closes down and creates depression. Without the clarity of the third eye we have no connection to ourselves, consciousness and all that is.

There are two members of the amphibian family that have gifts for us. One is a frog from the Amazon rainforest that creates a substance that is a neurotoxin. When taken it clears our body of poison mentally, physically and spiritually. I have taken this substance in South America and its detoxing properties are extraordinary. I don't think there's much chance of getting addicted to Kambo as it's called as one could hardly call the experience pleasurable but the after effects certainly are. This beautiful frog is a gift of detoxification for us. There is another amphibian from the Mexican Senora desert which is called The Toad. There is a substance in the saliva of these toads that is called Buffo containing 5-MeO-DMT or the 'god particle'. It is something that must be taken with very qualified expert shamans and although extraordinarily enlightening, it could create the opposite, if taken in the wrong way.

67

Many people ask me about addiction. In my experience, all addiction goes back to a sense of something missing that has been mirrored through our epigenetics and our other lives, reflected in our experience conception to three. If we have been in any way abused, abandoned or confused at this time, we will have a tendency through this trauma repeating itself to want something to take the pain away.

It is quite normal for human beings to want to eat when hungry and to partake of some of the fresh alcohol and medicinal plants and psychotropics as part of being a part of nature. I remember visiting an African village on the border of Uganda and Kenya where the Christians had not arrived and I was there for the ceremony for the arrival of some twins. The older women of the village would prepare fresh alcohol for the ceremony of planting and harvesting and for special occasions. I arrived for the celebration of the twins and after getting very drunk and enjoying themselves, they would have no alcohol for another six months.

The alcohol was fresh and they would not ferment it with sugar to store it as we do. The alcohol was very much part of a ceremony to connect with nature. The shamans of the village would do readings and everyone would have a good time with no violence or unhappiness. The problem with us is that we have available alcohol every day of the year with the explicit use of relieving our tension, boredom or depression, to make us feel more confident or to take us away from our misery. They didn't use the alcohol for anything but as a ceremony to the land and to their idea of a higher power which we call God.

I do believe that the original people of this earth had a relationship to everything that we use for addiction in the same way. We have used sexuality, reliance on other people, alcohol, narcotics, work, food, our devices and even stress as an addiction. If any of us use anything every day to get by, we have to seriously think whether we have an addictive relationship to it. If someone is overwhelmed by a relationship or their use of cocaine or alcohol a good place to start, if you're really serious about giving up, is with 12 step programmes within a fellowship such as Alcoholics Anonymous or Narcotics Anonymous.

Other people use a series of daily practices to break themselves out of addiction and continue with determination. So for example, if at 6pm you have a habit of having a drink, that needs to be broken by a yoga class, run, cup of tea, meditation or a warm bath. Around all addiction is something I call PPT (people, places and things).

If you've been used to taking cocaine every weekend with a particular bunch of people, you may need to break away from those people for a bit. If there's a particular time of day with a particular device with a particular mood that leads you to porn you must change your relationship to that set of circumstances. If you have a particular relationship to eating ice cream at night, you need to make damn sure there's no ice cream in your fridge - and let everyone around you know.

If you're used to getting to sleep with marijuana I suggest you go switch to CBD oil and meditation until you have broken the habit. If you are addicted to stress to keep you going, very slowly through meditation and walking you can start to calm your system down. Being addicted to stress is one of the hardest to recognise and you may well need a weekly process therapy to help you. I think we are all painfully aware of our addiction to devices and really our device is going to mirror back to us our own shadow so rather than throw your phone to the other side of the room, try to have a healthier relationship to how you use it, when you use it and why you use it.

Like any addiction you have to lessen your relationship with it and learn how to use it as a tool, stopping it being your master. Deepak Chopra claims it takes 21 consecutive days to make or break a habit.

68

In the past few centuries, literal thinking – rationalism and the traditional left brain binary thinking have run creative, intuitive right brain thought into the ground. Shamanic thinking can be a way to reconnect with the more creative, experiential side of ourselves. But what we know about neuroplasticity shows that in order to allow our 'right brain' creativity and intuitive wisdom to flourish, we need to practice using it. Starting small is key, and we all need some inspiring ways in.

True shamanism is the living experience of the inside-outside path. In other words when you realise that you are the creator and the influencer you realise that everything outside of you is talking to the inside of you and vice versa. When this clicks, you no longer view life experiences, your environment or your relationships as offering either rewards or punishment.

I had a true example of our environment talking to us the other day when I had an upsetting incident with my eldest daughter that ended up with me crying and feeling my heart would break. I allowed myself to go fully into this feeling as it seemed important, even though my higher self knew it was okay. In the morning I woke up and my Aga was stone cold. In my life this is a disaster because the Aga is the heart of the house. My friend and I soon realised that the fuse had burnt out on the Aga and we had no fuses to replace it with. Soon after there was a knock on the door and an electrician walked through the door. He had actually come to say hello as he was doing a job for my daughter who lives next door. He mended the Aga straight away and then noticed some burn marks around my down lights on the ceiling and said, "Wendy, that's a potential fire hazard". He showed me how moths and flies and all sorts were trapped in the lights. By the end of the day, he had replaced every downlighter in the house saving me £900 a year in energy costs. I resolved things with my daughter from the gift of the Aga mirroring back to me what I needed to understand.

If you really pay attention to what's going on around you, even if events seem out of your hands, like a bus being late or a valuable customer suddenly cancelling their contract, you will see how your environment is teaching you and be grateful for it.

I have mentioned transference and countertransference with other human beings but the same can be said in relation to our environment; we need to be more aware of how our environment influences us and how we influence our environment. Everything is a constant mirror and it's good to try and understand how it works.

69

In our culture we have a profoundly dysfunctional relationship with death. We are terrified of it. Death is sanitised, pushed to the edges of society and our thinking. It is institutionalised and de-humanised. Many old people are so isolated in the years approaching death that they are forced into a state of near-death emotionally. In contrast, many other cultures and not just tribal ones, have a far healthier, more integrated relationship to death.

I believe that in contrast, our fear of death leads to the same clinging in life that fuels codependency. In this sense, it is at the heart of our problems. We need to re-think death to move beyond this fear. Indigenous people are not concerned about death except in the moment of death. They don't live to avoid death as we do.

Watching various kinds of deer grazing on the African grasses, I have often observed with wonder, how calm they are even though yesterday a few of their family members and friends got eaten by a lion. Still, they munch away on grasses revelling in their environment. Only when one of them smells a lion and puts out the signal of danger, do they run and run as fast as they can, swivelling expertly on their back legs avoiding thorn bushes like ballet dancers. Finally, the lion singles out one of them and at the point of death you watch the deer surrender to its fate.

We on the other hand, in response to the stress of modern life, are often locked into a pattern of 'fear, flight and fight' and high adrenaline. Even when safe in our homes, we feel uneasy and scramble for a sense of calm by scrolling through our phones, flicking through the TV or perhaps reaching for alcohol, tobacco, stronger drugs or porn. The answer is to spend more time in nature, meditation, creative pursuits and healing modalities that keep us in a balanced rhythm.

Rather than remembering our dead in a big sentimental ceremonial gesture and forgetting about it, it is important to continue to remember them in our lives. Indigenous people see death as a doorway someone has gone through to a more useful place where they can help us. They remember them on an altar that they feed everyday with incense, fire, candles and bits of food. To them the ancestors are here as much as they are in a body.

Indigenous people say that what you are afraid of will stalk you. The animal world has a very different attitude to death. As I have just mentioned, a deer will use all its life force and adrenaline to escape death but at the point of death, it will surrender to its inevitability. The deer is not fearful of whether it will go to hell or heaven.

70

My journey so far has been experimenting with recreating some of the models of tribal life with my family and friends to create a new society that can remember our true relationship to each other and nature.

Creating a small community is first and foremost an inside-outside task. We all know what it feels like to be standing at a rainy bus stop with friends that we are in cahoots with – the late bus and the rain doesn't bother us because the sense of camaraderie with each other is so strong. It forces us into the moment.

In the same way, we know what it feels like to be on a beautiful beach with people we are at odds with - the beautiful beach cannot make up for the sense of alienation when we are not aligned or stuck in negative transference that triggers our inner pain. This means that to live in a community we must know our inner selves to know others. This work is essential to ensure we are able to get along. Each individual's willingness to understand themselves via the right kind of process work is the mainstay of a small community.

People often come to visit me in my home. Because it is a very idyllic place, they ask me questions like, How much did this cost you?. I laugh because it has literally been a journey of blood, sweat and tears with many people coming and going for fifty odd years and no real plan as to how it was going to evolve into what it is today.

Living in nature is to me the only way of living that makes sense. Each day you are relating to the plant, tree and animal family, that are always constant and kind. Even though human beings are extraordinary we have very much been going in a direction of complete selfishness. This has happened from being raised in a way that does not encourage caring enough about our environment or each other. When you live with a group of people you are constantly learning about yourself. Even though the community allows in some ways more time for oneself, to live naturally is hard work.

Once you have lived in that balance you learn to absolutely love it. Returning to a single selfish life is often too much to bear. I have found that people who have lived here, sometimes have to leave to find themselves. They always return because of the true magic that happens when you live in nature, with trees, children and animals. In other words, if you are going to live in the way that I am hoping to inspire you to live, be prepared for inner and outer hard work. Every day in all the seasons, there is wood to be collected, animals to be fed, and plants to be tended to. There is constant maintenance on the buildings and food to be collected and brought to the table. There is always a lot to do when you live in nature and this makes you feel connected everyday. Proper relationships require effort and truth and living with a group of people constantly brings out our less shiny sides to be healed. I wouldn't have it any other way. I know that anyone else who has lived with us here has experienced it as a very precious part of their healing journey.

71

Technology needs to be used for us, not against us. I firmly believe that technology can set us free to live as we should if it's used in the right way. Through technology, we can find our local community, even if we are living in separate homes. Once you have found a group with aligned values, one of you could have a larger space for you all to gather for communal meals. I suggest two a week, like Sunday brunch, and another evening in the week, where you all bring food and cook together, making a ceremony out of the meal. This can become a party with music, dancing and sharing of ideas. People with children and the people without children who want to be aunts and uncles, grandparents and grandmothers can offer support around the interaction with the children. Once a week or definitely once a month the small community can discuss with a talking stick about how they can support each other, and have fun, even if it has to be outside. It takes a lot of different colours to make a rainbow, and our differences are often our inspiration. It is helpful to have an older person who is happy to guide and keep space, but it is not necessary. Depending on our character some people are natural leaders but have to be careful that they don't set themselves up for too much responsibility. If the wish to share is there and the hearts are open, the right interaction can be achieved. I thoroughly recommend that you find a small green space, even if it is in one person's garden that you all take care of and grow food in. It would be nice if it was a common space that you could share the cost of, like an allotment. If that is not possible it doesn't really matter if it is one person's garden if you don't evaluate your effort in a monetary way that is benefiting someone else.

72

Consciousness, like nature, likes us to flow and grow. It does not tolerate stagnation and entropy. To truly live we have to get beyond the anxiety of death and face our worst fears to see the light. If we do this, we will be more able to be present to our daily experience, and find life a journey of beauty. By and large, worrying about the future creates anxiety and regretting the past creates depression. Being present creates harmony.

If we are going to think about the future we should allot proper time to think about it in a positive way with ceremonies, mood boards and planning. What we do here is have a big pin board with pictures of our ancestors as an ancestral healing space with plants, candles and crystals that can be charged with intention. This may seem peculiar in today's setting.

Whenever you are performing a ceremony, laughter and joy are very important components. Watching Indigenous people in ceremony is always full of laughter, singing and cooperation. Any kind of ceremony should be inclusive with everybody keeping space for everyone else, even if one person is leading.

Another mood board can be made with the community intentions around making gardens, growing food, building spaces and future fun with photographs, drawings and natural offerings from nature like feathers and flowers. If we are going to think about the past we need to do it in a therapeutic way, using process work to work some of the stuck past out of our systems. This leaves us more free to dream in a new future.

73

In all Indigenous tribes the women and the men go on gathering, hunting and fishing trips, often altogether. Although the children are mostly with them, if they do stay behind they do not feel the same abandonment as our children, because they are being left with people they have known since birth, and will know for the rest of their lives. It is very important that the children of a community feel connected in a heart space with the people that look after them. We need to explain to them exactly what is going on when members come and go into the outside world and do not take them with them. I often ask my clients who are 'content' but know that something is missing if they are aware of what that is.

Often they will tell me that they want a relationship or a nice house or a baby, not realising that they are externalising the feeling of emptiness that the way we live in separate boxes makes them feel. We have created a society that enables the narrative of being born in a hospital and then going to playgroup as early as one and a half or two. This is due to something called maternity care, which is sometimes the only way a couple can have a baby financially. The main narrative then supports their children going to a private or public primary school, secondary school and university.

At this university there is often an expectation of meeting the partner you may end up spending the rest of your life with, who you then buy a house with, get married and have children. The government and society do not support doing things in a completely different way which requires effort and thinking outside of the box.

If you have understood that a home birth is preferable to a hospital birth (as long as there are no complications) you will understand it's because the baby is going to be born into a dark candle lit space and beautiful music. Also only the people he has experienced from inside the womb will be at the birth with a loving midwife that the mother has met before. Sometimes of course a home birth is not possible, but if you are aware of the kind of welcome a child needs, even with a caesarian, the baby will experience a stress-free, welcoming arrival.

If in your heart you understand that somehow despite the financial implications and the difficulties of where to live, you really want to be able to spend as much time around your child with other like-minded and aligned individuals, you will somehow get together with other people to create a kind of community I'm writing about.

The most important thing is that intention creates flow and abundance. If we feel 'I'll never be able to do this' then we won't be able to. If we imagine a supportive environment we can manifest it. I know this is possible because I have literally manifested the impossible from having no property, no money and only debt.

Finding support, through people who feel the same way you do is key here. I know it's possible because I've done it, despite it being very hard to find people who think the same way as I do. If you then feel that the way normal school operates with the separation from adults to children in peer groups, with lessons only lasting at most an hour, so that the subject is not explored in depth with all of the senses, then you can set up your own school. All you need is one other like-minded parent with a child and the sitting room is your school with one good tutor. You can then create after school and weekend clubs. Then if you feel that to live in a nuclear family without the help of elders and other people around you doesn't make sense, then you can either live very close to your family if they are aligned with you, or make a family out of other like-minded people.

If there is an innate trust at the centre, absences can be covered. If you have separate homes or pods around a central space, then if someone wants to leave, they could sell their pod to someone else who is aligned to the principles of the community. It is sometimes good for the group to have fresh input from new people, the members who are from eighteen to thirty are to be expected to want to move away, and usually the members over thirty five or with children would perhaps stay, but everyone is different.

Here I bought the land and built everything on it until recently, when others have put some money in. We thought it was best to put the whole property in just one name before creating a trust. There are many ways to set up the actual land and properties. The most important thing is to have a sacred relationship with each other and the land kept alive and fluid with ceremony and with each other.

It is vital that you are all aligned on the basis of knowing yourself with process work so you can call each other out on transferences and insecurities. It is vital that you share the same ideas around childcare, education and the care of the land. It is vital that you appreciate each other's strengths and weaknesses.

74

The world is finally realising about the principle of the 'terrain not the symptom', which applies to the world itself and our own bodies. One of the biggest reasons for climate change and the destruction of species at such a fast rate is that we polluted and denuded our soil. Many enlightened farmers, and NGOs are realising that we must feed our soil and many people have begun to understand that true health lies in having a healthy body. Everyday I try to educate people that we must think of the terrain not the symptom. The symptom is a way of the body alerting us to the imbalance at the core of the body. It's the way our body is trying to tell us that something isn't quite right. Yet we still trot off to the doctor for a pill to take away the warning signal. If our car showed a red oil light, I don't think we'd want to turn it off, we'd want to fill it up with oil. But if our lower back hurts, we want to take a pill to make the pain go away rather than realise that our lower back represents our support structure and any pain indicates an imbalance mentally, physically, emotionally, spiritually.

Likewise, we are realising that we need to correct the imbalance that intensive animal farming, constant spraying of chemicals and agribusiness have done and return the soil to its original state. Only then will the vegetables and the animals grazing on the ground be in a healthy state. We then, as consumers of the vegetables and the animals will be in a healthy state.

The same goes for the seas and the rivers. Healthy soil is key to the survival of everything. Zac Bush is the best person I have listened to and read about on this very important subject. There are many wonderful projects around the world that you can search for on the internet. Where we live, we have dug for water and we make compost out of a mixture of leaves, weeds, dried human faeces (separate from urine) and food waste.

We need to understand that the way we deal with human faeces is very wasteful in terms of water use. For millennia people used animal and human faeces to make compost and understood intrinsically that the only time there is a smell or disease is when the urine and faeces are mixed together.

My first lesson in this was when I visited China and in the old houses the night soil man would come and collect the human faeces that was separate to the urine and did not smell. The men would urinate separately to the women and this was collected for particular plants and was paid for as a valuable compost for the vegetables. If you dilute urine by 1:3 it is a valuable fertilizer. You can read all about this in a book called *Liquid Gold*. The toilets that we have in Bath separate urine from faeces and dry the faeces with a fan. People are amazed that they don't smell.

The subject of personal health has become a very important subject. The dictionary definition of the word 'sovereign' is 'independent', autonomous, self-governing and free. I believe each human being would love to understand more about how they could know their own health, mentally and physically. I think people would love to know how to connect to their own intuition, their own heart and knowing themselves. I am against glyphosate which has crept into our food chain which is extremely bad for our health and bodies.

Glyphosate is the unpleasant ingredient used in agri-business and on quite a few gardens in the western world. We have degraded the soil in which we grow our food and graze our animals and we have degraded the soil of our bodies. I have experienced and firmly believe that it is the overall health of our bodies and minds that is much more important than targeting a symptom with an overall drug which will cause more symptoms, which will need to be treated by more medication in a vicious cycle leading to more and more ill health.

The way that viruses affect the human body is quick and sometimes extreme but when the body has dealt with the virus through the immune system, the body is always stronger. The only time a virus will actually kill its host is when the host is extremely weak from other symptoms. Viruses are a natural part of nature and have always been part of how we live and die. Far more people die of heart attacks, diabetes, and cancer, than have died of viruses. I feel it is up to every individual to be in charge of their own health and seek medical health where they feel necessary, but it is always a personal choice. If somebody feels scared and vulnerable then they must protect themselves but they have no right to tell other people what to do.

We all need to understand how the body mind spirit works by delving deep into the old ways of looking at health. The old fashioned doctor who went house to house with his black bag knew that little Tommy had a tummy ache because his mother had had a baby. These days, the ear, nose and throat doctor does not talk to the hip doctor and there is no coordinated health criteria for each individual with a lot of wasted time, money and disappointed patients.

The beautiful art of 5-Element Acupuncture that I practice treats the entire body mind and spirit and connects all three up in a person's understanding of their body. This puts them on a road to true health. I once had a dream of opening clinics everywhere in the world that were half alternative and half medical; they would be free clinics and people would queue up to be seen by a medical doctor first. If they could be treated by alternative means they would be sent to the alternative clinic. If they had a life-threatening disease like advanced pneumonia they would be given antibiotics and be sent to the advisory part of the alternative clinic to teach them different methods to safeguard their lungs. I managed to open one in Africa that was very successful. It is still a dream I would like to realise worldwide when the people themselves understand that this is what would serve them best.

75

When I was eighteen, I took a job in Greece at eighteen along with my best friend as a cook in a rental villa. I showed my father the ad in the paper and he said it looked very dodgy. I thought he was being boring and restrictive. Off we set to our destination on a Greek island with no real knowledge of where we were going and we definitely didn't know how to cook. The owner of the villa turned out to be indeed quite a sketchy figure.

He had many debts on the villa, including for the boat which had been put under my name and passport to which I had innocently agreed before we started the job. He had banked the guests' money and disappeared. This money was meant to buy food and supplies for the guests, the villa and our wages. Of course this did not happen!

We fed the first guests on rice and herbs and they were not happy. I sent a telegram (no internet in those days) to the very capable boyfriend I had just broken up with saying 'Help! Urgent! Please come immediately'. He turned up somehow three days later and we made a plan. Being thoroughly capable he decided we should use the boat for waterskiing lessons for other tourists in the village, using the money to buy food for our guests. This worked for a while until various electricity and gas companies started turning up for their money. My ex-boyfriend needed to get back to his job. That left me in a bit of a pickle as I was responsible for the debt of the boat. I managed to persuade some fishermen to smuggle me out at night to Brindisi.

These are the moments of rock bottom despair that are extremely useful because the only way is up. You truly face the prospect of death and something happens that makes you break through to possibility. You don't need anything as extreme as this experience to know that if you stop and go very deep, there is always help for you from what many call God and I call our connection to consciousness. I sat on that train station bench feeling angry, rejected, frightened, ashamed, sad and stupid. A little voice inside me said 'just breathe because breath is free and available to all'. From that moment in that station all sorts of things happened that led me back home a little wiser.

76

I cannot emphasize enough how important it is to realize that there is no failure at any time. All the most interesting people I have known have had colourful lives. All the happiest people I have known have faced death, pain and loss, to truly live. They came to realize you have to accept who you choose to be in this lifetime. They learned to love their perceived flaws whether it is a large nose, short legs, dyslexia or blindness. They learned they are an energy field in a body, in this space time reality and that is a glorious gift if they can accept it. They learn that they will be many people in many bodies in many lifetimes and that all is meant to be.

If we can understand all of our emotions and traumas in this manner and process them accordingly to this mindset, we will find a way to navigate our way through life and relationships, even if some of the time it feels very difficult.

Death is part of life, but when we accept its inevitability, we know how precious life is. I lost one of my best friends when I was in my early twenties. He had a very obvious crush on me, which I selfishly ignored because I loved the attention, but with hindsight, I was unable to return his love in the same way. We were extremely close and shared many wonderful times and in a way I took his love for granted. When I refused to return his calls, after meeting my first husband, who had told me I was being selfish by staying friends with him, a terrible thing happened. He got very drunk with my brother and drove his car into a brick wall and died instantly. Guilty and ashamed I had a complete breakdown and lost three months of my life in a cut off altered state of grief.

After three months in this state, I experienced a profound coming back into my body and my brain and started to forgive myself and carry on with life. I was far more aware after that of other people's feelings.

The second death that marked me was the death of my forty year old beloved younger brother, followed shortly by the death of both our parents. After that triple loss, in a short time frame, I had no family left that I was close to. When my brother died, I wanted to die and could not bear the pain. I only carried on because of my children. I became anxious when driving that I would drive off the road and kill myself as the grief was so enormous, so intense. My brother died of cancer and at this time, I developed cancer myself. I made a complete change in my life and moved to Kenya and my body healed itself without drugs.

In time, I processed death and I now know that if anyone close to me dies I can let them go knowing we are always connected, just not in a body. The worst thing that I have encountered in myself and others is denial. Bringing anything that is difficult to the surface, especially with a kind witness, even if it is a cat, a dog or a tree will help, and all trauma can heal.

77

If you watch water it is extraordinary how it flows where it wants to flow and life is often like this. We can make something like a water drain and then be very surprised when a rock falling into the drain allows the water to spill all over the place. We can set up a garden and expect a fantastic crop of carrots when unexpectedly some carrot blight takes them all. We can presume that our relationships are rock solid and nothing is going to change them when one person suddenly, like water, flows off into another direction and our daily experience of them has to change. We have to be flexible and allow the natural constant of change to be in our lives. If we meditate together and separately, we can realise that there is some divine plan. This way we can trust that movement is natural at all times, and that no decision can be a wrong decision. It is just part of learning.

Afterword

In the run-up to celebrating my 70th birthday, I felt a calling to write this book, primarily hoping to encourage readers to copy nature and keep in flow. Separated from the readily available gifts of nature we have been operating for a very long time from fear of loss and insecurity and this has made us invest in staying safe and not truly living. We are meant to experience life as a journey, like Frodo Baggins in Lord of the Rings. Life, like the ring, has the ability to take us into the shadow or the light. It is up to us, via a willingness to face death to learn how to truly live. I hope this book in some part inspires you to have the courage to keep moving and changing as nature does, learning as you go, that the only constant is LOVE.

Acknowledgements

Thank you Gail Rebuck, Nick Johnstone, Helena Warwick Cross, Henry Gibbs, Robin Pigott, Tim Spiller, Lawrie Millar, Rebecca James, Nalina Giacopazzi, Chris Shaw, Vanessa Kirby, Lucy Ormerod and Benjamin Benstead.